10

Secrets for a Happy Marriage

. . ❀ *. .*

10

Secrets for a Happy Marriage

＊.₰.＊ ❀ ＊.₰.＊

Compiled by
Carma B. Sirrine

CFI
Springville, Utah

ISBN 13: 978-1-59955-196-8

Published by CFI, an imprint of Cedar Fort, Inc., 2373 W. 700 S., Springville, UT 84663
Distributed by Cedar Fort, Inc., www.cedarfort.com

LIBRARY OF CONGRESS CATALOGING-IN-PUBLICATION DATA

Sirrine, Carma B.
  10 Secrets for a Happy Marriage / Carma B. Sirrine.
    p. cm.
  ISBN 978-1-59955-196-8 (acid-free paper)
  1. Marriage--Religious aspects--Church of Jesus Christ of Latter-day
Saints. 2. Man-woman relationships--Religious aspects--Church of Jesus
Christ of Latter-day Saints. 3. Marriage--Religious aspects--Mormon Church.
I. Title.
  BX8641.S555 2008
  248.8'44--dc22
                            2008026832

Cover design by Jen Boss
Cover design © 2009 by Lyle Mortimer
Edited and typeset by Heidi Doxey

Printed in the United States of America

10 9 8 7 6 5 4 3 2 1

Printed on acid-free paper

Acknowledgments

I would like to especially thank the friends who answered early and well. They gave me the courage to continue on with this literary endeavor. Among those sharing a part of their life with us are authors, wives of doctors, business executives, a music personality, religious leaders, nurses, educators, loving wives and mothers, insurance personnel, retired couples, and businessmen and women.

I thank my husband, Gordon, for his patience while I was working at my computer at all hours and for his love and devotion to me and my dreams. I also thank my children and grandchildren for their belief in my ability to really make a difference through the compiling of this book.

I also want to thank my publisher, Cedar Fort. Thank you to Jeffrey Marsh for his first email saying that Cedar Fort wanted to publish my book. That was very exciting. And for his encouragement along the way. More thanks to two editors who helped me correct a few mistakes or typos that are no longer there. Heather Holm for helping me greatly in knowing where the book stood time-wise and so forth. I thank Heidi Doxey, my final editor, for her expertise in making the book all come together. The editorial board also has my deep gratitude for realizing that this book is one of a kind for all readers and can make a significant change in many lives.

Every person and marriage is different, but all are elevated by applying the proven principles of patience, good communication, unconditional love, forgiveness, commitment, unselfishness, and sacrifice. In *10 Secrets for a Happy Marriage*, Carma Sirrine has been able to express these key components of a good marriage through real-life stories. She has taken a practical approach to inspire healthy and happy relationships. Surely, everyone will find ways to improve their marriage when reading this book, if only to remind us of things that have become lost from our attention. I know I did.

Senator Wayne L. Niederhauser

Utah State Senate, District 9

Reading Carma Sirrine's book was delightful, thought-provoking, and thoroughly absorbing. This collection of stories from real-life marriages rings true, as each is written by individual spouses from their own experience. I was amazed at the variety of successful marriages and the many differing principles that were shared for happiness in these relationships. Obviously, no two marriages are alike, but many solutions to the problems most marriages experience are shared here. Innovative ideas for improving relationships are also found in this book.

At a time when the definition of marriage is being argued, and the institution itself is being questioned, I found evidence on every page that not just good marriages, but great marriages exist in numerous homes. My beliefs were reconfirmed that with effort, ingenuity, and help from our Heavenly Father, marriage can be a source of eternal happiness. Working on that important relationship is essential, and this book can be a wonderful resource. Kudos to Carma for her efforts to find and put into print these many examples of how to improve our marriage relationships!

Elaine Wright Christensen

Utah Poet of the Year, 1990; author of two prize-winning collections: *At The Edges* and *I Have Learned 5 Things*.

Table of Contents

. . ❁ *. .*

Foreword

. . ❁ *. .*

BY LARRY W. TIPPETTS, PHD,
AUTHOR OF *A Practical Guide on the Moral Issue*

Following the completion of an advanced degree in family relations in 1973, I was assigned to teach a preparation for marriage course at the LDS institute of religion where I was employed. I have continued to teach marriage classes for nearly thirty-five years. My experience as a teacher and my own marriage of forty years has impressed upon me the crucial importance of marriage and family life. No arena of life has a more direct impact on our overall happiness and contentment than does our family.

President Hinckley once said, "I am concerned about family life in the Church. We have wonderful people, but we have too many whose families are falling apart. It is a matter of serious concern. *I think it is my most serious concern.*"[1]

Carma Sirrine, a wife, mother, grandmother, and friend, has put together a practical and inspirational collection of real life stories and statements from dozens of husbands, wives, couples, sons, and daughters, who have experienced the joys and weathered the storms of family life. This book helps to address President Hinckley's concern about marriage by providing practical examples that couples can emulate in their own efforts to build eternal families.

The reader will find within these pages the most common problems of married life that too many commonly use as a justification for depression or conflict, and that often lead to the divorce court. Yet the vast majority of these couples remained happily married.

What made the difference?

One of the themes revealed in this helpful book is an attitude of, "we will work it out," an optimistic "stick-to-itiveness" that enabled these couples to keep trying. Several mention that they would simply never discuss divorce. In a recent general conference, Elder Dallin H. Oaks reported on a body of research indicating two out of three unhappily married couples who avoided divorce reported being happily married five years later![2]

Marriage and family life is difficult. In a sense it is a laboratory for godhood. It has been said that marriage and parenthood are not only the sources of our greatest joys, but also the sources of our greatest pains and failures. We delight in the joys but somehow conclude that we should be exempt from the pain. Someone once quipped that marriage is like a three-ring circus: First comes the engagement ring, then the wedding ring, and last of all the suffer-ring.

Actually, difficulty is one of our greatest teachers, and therefore, our greatest friend. This is a difficult lesson to grasp, and one that may not be fully appreciated until after the trials have been endured well. This principle is taught most clearly in the scriptures—in fact, there are few themes that are taught more frequently in the standard works or in general conference than the value of adversity in making us more like God.

I recently visited in the hospital with a retired couple whose lives were abruptly turned upside down by a diagnosis of cancer. Formerly active and involved in multiple full-time missions, they now face greatly reduced mobility and the very real possibility of death. And yet I could not help but sense the increased levels of love and devotion which flowed from that otherwise disappointing circumstance. Whether it be health challenges, financial stress, children who break parent's hearts, parents who break children's hearts, or any of a number of circumstances that now face couples and families—all of these things shall give us experience and can be turned to our eventual good (D&C 90:24; Romans 8:28).

Marriage and family life will include an abundant mixture of pleasure and pain, good and bad, delight and despair. During a particularly difficult time in our family life I came across these lines by William Blake about joy and woe. I found them strangely comforting. I typed them on a card and carried them with me for several years, reading it frequently enough that I now quote it from memory.

> Joy and woe is woven fine,
> A clothing for the soul divine.
> Under every grief and pine
> Runs a joy with silken twine.
> It is right, it should be so:
> Man was made for joy and woe;
> And when this we rightly know
> Through the world we safely go.[3]

One of the clearest statements I have ever found on the importance of family life was written by Elder Neal A. Maxwell over thirty years ago. Each time I read these words, I understand more fully why marriage can be difficult:

> A good member of the Church must understand the implications of his beliefs with regard to the home. This different commitment will mean, among many things, knowing
> —that because the home is so crucial, it will be the source of our greatest failures as well as our greatest joys.
> —that home is the one place we will be in that will require us to practice every major gospel principle and not just a few, as may be the case in some temporary relationships.
> —that the pressures of life in a family will mean that we shall be known as we are, that our frailties will be exposed and, hopefully, we shall then work on them.
> —that the love and thoughtfulness required in the home are no abstract exercise in love. They are real. It is no mere rhetoric concerning some distant human cause; it is an encounter with raw selfishness, with the need for civility and taking turns, of being hurt and yet forgiving, of being at the mercy of others' moods and yet understanding, in part, why we sometimes inflict pain on each other.
> —that family life is a constant challenge, not a periodic performance we can render on a stage quickly and run for the privacy of a "dressing room" to be alone with ourselves, for the home gives us a great chance to align our public and private behavior, to reduce the hypocrisy in our lives, to be more congruent with Christ.[4]

One of the strengths of this book are the short, to-the-point case studies that enable us to see more clearly the principles that lead to the resolution of differences and the attainment of happiness. For example,

- One couple resolved early on never to yell at one another.
- Another describes the challenges of blending two families.
- We read of the faith of an elderly couple to fulfill a mission despite many setbacks and obstacles.
- The mother who "ran away from home."
- How a family turned a ninety-mile round trip to the meetinghouse three to five times each week into a positive blessing that unified their family.
- Learning how to change expectations.
- A wife jealous of her husband's time as bishop.
- Another wife jealous of her husband's time hunting.

If a couple were to read these case studies aloud to one another (one reads while the other gives the reader a foot rub), and then discuss the principles and practices together, it would turn into a very practical (and inexpensive) form of marriage therapy. There are literally dozens of great ideas for solving problems within the pages of this book.

To younger readers some of these accounts may seem a bit "old-fashioned." Many were written by couples who have survived the storms of life and are looking back and reminiscing on the ups and downs of marriage and family life. The old-fashioned verities of commitment, responsibility, working hard, forgiving, and trusting in God really work! Young married couples face a different world and a different set of challenges, but the principles essential for growth and happiness have not changed. I wish I had been exposed to some of the great ideas in this book during the formative years of my own marriage.

As a married couple ages they accumulate a storehouse of memories. The importance of good memories cannot be over-emphasized. Even the painful and difficult experiences can be reframed by remembering rightly—seeing those experiences through the mind of God. My heart aches for those who grow up in troubled, broken homes, or who experienced abuse at the hands of family members. Mothers and fathers would do well to consider the words of Father Zossima, an admirable character in one of Dostoyevsky's novels:

> From the home of my childhood I have brought nothing but precious memories, for there are no memories more precious than those of early childhood in one's first home. And that is almost always so if there

is any love and harmony in the family at all. Indeed, precious memories may remain even of a bad home, if only the heart knows how to find what is precious.[5]

The value of family and home life is to shape us for eternity! Even the painful experiences can minister to us in ways that we cannot comprehend. No other experience in mortality will prepare us so well to accomplish the purposes for which we were placed on this earth. This book will help by giving the reader a broader perspective of what marriages and families can be, and provide dozens of practical ways that this ideal can be achieved.

Notes

1. Dell Van Orden, "President Hinckley Notes His 85th Birthday," *Church News*, 24 June 1995, 6, emphasis added.
2. Dallin H. Oaks, "Divorce," *Ensign*, May 2007, 73.
3. William Blake, *The Complete Poetry and Prose of William Blake* (New York: Doubleday, 1988), 494–95.
4. Neal A. Maxwell, "The Value of Home Life," *Ensign*, Feb. 2007, 7.
5. Fyodor Dostoyevsky, *The Brothers Karamozov* (New York: Barnes & Noble Books, 1995), 268.

Introduction

*. *. * ❁ *. *. *

This book was conceived after much pondering and praying about a subject I could write on that could and would be successful. While on our senior service mission for the LDS Church to the Philippines during 1999 and 2000, my husband and I realized what a wonderful group of senior missionaries we were privileged to know. These couples were devoted to each other and to the work they had been called to accomplish. Because of the associations we made there, which continue to this day, I decided to write a book about having a successful marriage.

I decided to contact in person, by telephone, or through email many of the friends and acquaintances I had made over the years. Yes, I even included a few relatives as well. They were all told that I was compiling a book of stories and experiences from couples I knew and that their knowledge of how to be successful in marriage would be delightful for others to read.

After receiving most of the material, I divided it into ten separate chapters—each with a different focus on marriage. (Several experiences could have been in two or three different chapters.) I found that not all marriages were perfect from the beginning, but for the most part, the couples whose stories make up this book worked hard to stay together and succeeded. Some couples made commitments from the very beginning about how they would conduct their marriage and give their children the care and nurturing they would deserve. Some couples had a situation arise that changed their marriage for the better. And some of the couples were unable to cope with unhappy situations and divorced, only to have a great second marriage.

What I want to accomplish with this book is foster the desire and commitment in those who read it to renew their efforts to have a happier, more productive marriage. Those who are not married can also gain insight into some of the habits they can change in themselves to be more ready for marriage and to help them look for the right attributes in a future spouse.

1

Rely on The Lord

"Counsel with the Lord in all thy doings, and he will direct thee for good; yea, when thou liest down at night lie down unto the Lord, that he may watch over you in your sleep; and when thou risest in the morning let thy heart be full of thanks unto God; and if ye do these things, ye shall be lifted up at the last day." (Alma 37:37)

.❀. ❀ *.❀.*

The following story shows what a spiritual advantage the writer had while praying daily for protection and remembering the advice given in his patriarchal blessing.

"Sit in that chair and don't move!" is a statement I will never forget. In the spring of 1953, I had a patriarchal blessing that has helped me all my life. The patriarch was an older man, probably in his late eighties. This blessing was given on a Sunday morning at his home. I was in my final months of college at Utah State University in Logan, Utah. I knew that soon I would be entering the Air Force as I was in the ROTC program and would be a commissioned second lieutenant in the Air Force. I had told the patriarch of my plans. As part of my patriarchal blessing, the patriarch promised me a great blessing if I would live so as to have the Holy Ghost with me in my life. He told me that I would be warned of hidden dangers that would confront me. The Holy Ghost would warn me of these hidden dangers that could take my life. The patriarch said

I should listen and if I acted according to the warnings, I would be rendered safe from these dangers.

While in the Air Force, I received several of those warnings and my life was saved as a result of my being made aware of these dangers. On one such occassion, my wife and I had gone to Atlanta, Georgia in the early seventies to a school board convention. I was president of the local board of education. The convention was being held at a new Hyatt Hotel in Atlanta. One of the features of this hotel was that the rooms for the hotel were all built around the perimeter of the hotel, so that the inside was open with open hallways and balconies clear to the roof.

The hotel's size was quite spectacular—I believe it went up to thirty floors. The cashier's office was on the first floor, and folks had to stand in line for the office out in the open space. Near the cashier's office was a nice little stand or gazebo with brochures for other Hyatt hotels and many pamphlets for the sights of Atlanta. This was strategically placed and clearly arranged so that people could view the material while other members of their party checked out.

We had arranged with other members of our group to go down to the cashier's office to check out at noon. Vehicles would take us to the airport shortly after that time. At about ten minutes to noon, my wife and I were in our room just completing the packing of bags. We finished our packing and decided to have our customary prayer that we always have while traveling. I gave this prayer, and when I concluded instead of having bell boys come and get our suitcases, I decided that I could carry them down to the cashier's office. My wife was a little upset that I was carrying our heavy luggage.

We arrived down at the cashier's office about two minutes to noon. I took my wife and had her sit down in one of the chairs that faced toward this little gazebo filled with brochures. I was then prompted by the Holy Ghost to move my wife from this chair to one further away, under the overhang, and told her stay there until I got back from the cashier's office. She was a bit unhappy at being dictatorially told, "Sit in that chair and don't move!" (Especially since I had failed to tell her it was based on a prompting I had received.) Despite her unhappiness, she remained in that new chair I had placed her in. I turned and walked to the now vacant cashier area to begin my checkout. Then I heard a crash behind me. As I whirled around, I saw a heavy purse strike the gazebo, and within a second a woman's body landed on the floor right where my wife had been.

My wife was safe in her new chair just a few feet away. Hotel personnel quickly covered the dead woman with a canvas.

What would have happened to my wife, to our love, and our marriage if I had not listened to and acted upon the prompting of the Holy Ghost at that time? Most likely she would have been maimed or even killed. I thanked my Father in Heaven for this prompting.

My wife and I left Atlanta shaken by this experience but returned home to our fine family and continued our happy marriage. How blessed I felt that my wife had shared in the fruits of my wonderful patriarchal blessing.

In this story the couple relied on the Lord through prayer to help them make wise decisions. They gained experience and now feel that children should have the same opportunity for agency.

The very best thing that helped us with our marriage was to live across the country, away from family members. My husband and I are both from Maryland originally. When we married he was going to school on a Navy scholarship at the University of Utah. I worked at the LDS Hospital and that was our means of support while he was in school.

This was the best thing for our marriage because we were forced to work things out on our own and not rely on parents. If we had an argument, we worked it out instead of running home to mom and dad, seeking advice. It was at this time we investigated and joined The Church of Jesus Christ of Latter-day Saints. This decision has affected our lives for good in many wonderful ways. We were on our own with only Heavenly Father to counsel with unless we wanted to spend the money on a long-distance phone call to parents, and we had no money to do this.

I can't help but think that Heavenly Father sends us to earth to fend for ourselves—to learn, grow, and experience life on our own, though he's only a prayer away. We as parents need to allow our children the same agency. We can offer free advice with the promise that we won't be upset if they don't accept it. We often do not accept all of Heavenly Father's advice, but he's always there to pick us up and help us when we need him. He's only a prayer away.

This couple relied heavily on their marriage covenants made with the Lord. Journal writing provided their outlet for answers given through prayer and helped them remember those answers for future challenges.

During a particularly strenuous period in our lives, the pressures on our marriage relationship were very difficult. During that period we did two things that enabled us to regain or maintain our perspective. First, we relied heavily on the promises we made to each other in the temple when we were sealed. We both took our covenants very seriously and knew that ways would open up to ease the concerns we had. Second, we also continually asked ourselves what the Savior would have us do to resolve the challenges we were facing. Recorded in our journals are numerous specific instances of guidance, strength received, and numerous reminders that fortified our commitment to God, and consequently to each other. Together, we were able to weather discouraging circumstances because of the renewal we felt as a result of these two practices.

The husband in this story had a gradual "mighty change of heart," which changed his life to show the good attributes he possessed. He then used these attributes while serving as a senior missionary with his wife.

We faced a lot of issues during our many years of marriage, and there were many times when I wanted to give up and get a divorce because I just didn't think I could face trying to raise our children in the Church without much support from my husband. The main thing that got me through it all, besides a lot of prayer, was the knowledge that the "goodness" was still in him. I just had to have the patience for it to come back out. It was an amazing thing to watch as he had a "mighty change of heart" and slowly, but surely began to change.

Finally, after many years, we could talk about the Church and spiritual matters without it being a source of contention. I always loved him but didn't always like him. He truly has become converted, and it is wonderful to hear him talk to others about the gospel and testify to its truthfulness.

Yes, I have changed too. I've worked at being more patient and understanding and trying to keep my mouth shut when sometimes I want to speak out against something he says or does. We're still working on our marriage after all these years but have grown so much closer to each other since we've been on our mission. It was very hard at first, adjusting to being together nearly all the time. We've both seen a different side of each other as we teach the gospel to others and give service and comfort to those who are in need of it. We've increased in our knowledge of the principles of the gospel many times over what we thought we knew before.

God answered the prayers of this husband and father by giving him the opportunity to learn about himself. Listening to friends, relatives, and coworkers made a world of difference.

Everyone has his own story. We hope that what works for us may be applicable to others somehow.

Before we were married, we were taught correct principles from our parents. We communicated those needs we felt were of most importance. We committed to giving our relationship 110 percent. We also decided that if it wasn't working, it was our own fault. We decided that it takes two to make it work. After we wed we put God first. We decided that openness and trust were important. We learned that self-discipline would make us or break us. It did both. We had a tough time arguing. Rather than argue, it was easier to hold it in and not discuss the problem. We had to agree to argue. One person would sometimes have to persist until the other would talk. We invited the spirit into our disagreements with prayer. This really made a difference. Think about hearing the problem in third person and then seeing that desire as the other person petitioned the Lord for help. This is why it worked. God knows us and he knows what works.

We learned that communicating was sometimes impossible. At those times, prayer became an important part of bridging the gap.

I remember one time when I was especially frustrated because I realized that I didn't know my wife as well as I needed to, to be able to communicate with her effectively. I was very inadequate at realizing why my approach was all wrong. I used prayer to get help entering her heart and communicating what I felt was important. God heard it and softened her heart, and we talked. Surprisingly, this happened more than once! This worked quite well, to a point. Then, God answered my prayers differently. He gave me opportunities to educate myself about myself. I got feedback from fellow workers, family, and from school. It started to sound like what my wife was saying. It sounded like what my mom tried to teach me. I started to listen.

Listening made a big difference. Sometimes we discovered that we would still hurt each other. We discovered that what bothered us most was what we had to work on the most. So we made that our job—to recognize that weakness and work to perfect it. This is also how tasks around the house got done.

When the kids came (more than one at a time) this was a major trial. We were unprepared. We were scared and entertained a great deal of anxiety. Our lack of faith at first about killed us. We determined to not doubt and believe that everything would work out for the best. We often failed, but we prayed a lot and then we tried harder. We kept our commitments to God. We knew that if we did our part he would somehow bless us; he did.

Things were often not how we would have ordered them. We got help. It was never enough, but it was always more than we could possibly hope for. We saw major setbacks, and we saw progress as we met each setback. We are still progressing and meeting heavy resistance, so that is life.

What brings us together? We are both committed to making our marriage work. Getting together is something we don't do too often but we should! We let go of hard feelings by trying to separate ourselves from the problem. We are demanding of each other and of ourselves, yet we lower our expectations to what is realistic.

.❀. ❁ *.❀.*

How wonderful that this husband could earn a living doing something he really enjoyed. Beekeeping was for him. They attended the temple every week and maintained a program of self-reliance, which was a great example to their children.

My husband and I have been married sixty years. It has been quite a learning experience. He was a beekeeper. He started keeping bees when he was a senior in high school. His biology teacher got him interested. He asked his parents if he could get some beehives, and his mother said yes since her parents had some beehives. They bought ten hives from Montgomery Ward.

A local beekeeper found out my future husband was not afraid of bees and asked him to come and work for him and his son. Through the years he learned a lot about bees from them.

We were married in the fall of 1944. After World War II when trucks became available again, we bought a big two-ton truck, which I drove to and from and between beeyards while he slept. With this truck we could haul one hundred single-story hives to California to pollinate the almond trees. He worked the midnight shift for the Denver & Rio Grand Western Railroad for about twenty years. For another twenty he had the afternoon shift.

Our first little girl went across the Sierra Nevada Mountains from Salt Lake to west of Chico, California three times by the time she was one year old. Soon a baby boy joined our family and went with us also. During the next six years, our beehives accumulated from 250 to 1,500.

First, we put the hives in the orchards for pollination. We moved into mountain yards in the spring, starting around Mother's Day. Then to lower valleys in Box Elder and Weber Counties in Utah around the fourth of July. After extracting the honey during the last week of August and first week of September, we moved the hives to beeyards near our home for the winter where we could feed them and requeen in the spring.

We had two boys and two girls. Between them we have fifteen grandchildren and two great-grandchildren to bless our lives. Through the years we raised large gardens and cared for our fruit trees. We canned everything—vegetables and fruit. We tried to have a year's supply. We had a cow and sold milk. I made butter and cottage cheese. We raised steers, killed them, and then sold the meat, keeping some for ourselves. Now the steers and the bees are gone as it is too difficult for us to take care of them.

Through the years we have always been able to go one day a week to the temple. Now that we are older, we still go to the temple each week. It has been an interesting life with family and friends. We have no regrets at all. The Lord has always been with us to help us make good decisions. It has been a wonderful married life.

This couple feels that the Lord prepared them for each other. Their ideals and plans of an eternal family have changed over the years, but their eternal companionship has not changed.

Right from the start neither one even thought of a chance of failure.

The one thing that continually comes to my mind is something that my future wife and I did when we met. We had been writing to each other throughout my mission but had never met. On that night we drove up by the Logan temple and discussed what it was that we both wanted. We talked about an eternal family. Keep in mind we were not engaged at the time, but just getting to know each other. She told me while we were there that she wanted an eternal family and that going to the temple was very important to her. I knew from the way she said it that she was sincere and I really respected that. From that point on, we both treated our relationship like it might turn out that way.

It was only three weeks before we were engaged, but when I proposed to her I didn't ask her to marry me. I asked her if she wanted to have that eternal family that we had talked about. She said "Yes" and then I asked her if she would marry me. It has almost seemed in hindsight that the "marriage" part of it was subservient to something much more. The eternal companionship that we have has never been bound by marriage. We made a decision at the time, although subconsciously, that we were creating a bond that nothing could break.

The term *marriage* always seems to be rigidly defined. The opposite terminology speaks of "divorce" and "separation." The companionship that we created was above any definition. The Lord allowed us to be sealed under his power, and nothing that we, nor anyone else, can do can break that as long as we live our part. We both felt that the Lord had prepared us for each other and that even though we do have our quirks and differences, the marriage has never suffered because the companionship won't allow it.

This may all seem philosophical to some, but we have had our share of ups and downs. Trials with disease, finances, and wayward children have all taken their toll on us mentally and physically. Our view of the eternal family that we agreed to create has changed over the years, but we would both do it again if given the chance, and I would still ask the questions the same way. I believe that my wife would still say "Yes" just as emphatically as she did the first time. Right from the start neither one of us even thought of the chance of failure. Failure at life's challenges—yes, we knew there would be some, but we always knew that we would either suffer or rejoice together as one. It just doesn't seem possible to do it any other way.

Gratitude had graced this couple as they have relied on the Lord for assistance. They have the same goals, but life has been painful at times.

We will have been married for twenty-nine years next week. After discussing this subject and trying to figure out all the elements involved in our successful marriage, we decided it was very simple. We both have the same goals. We were sealed in the Oakland Temple for all time and eternity, and we both want to keep this covenant.

It has not been easy as life can be very painful at times. We have always stayed focused on our goal and stayed close to Heavenly Father. We have continued to try to grow and ask Heavenly Father for assistance. We are working on being more grateful and not taking ourselves too seriously. We have always taken the time to get away by ourselves a couple times a year so we can relax, enjoy our time together, and make lots of memories. We have worked on our family budget together so we both know what our finances are, and we make financial decisions together. The best way to get to know your spouse is to jump in the car and take a road trip. You will find out how many things you have in common and really learn about each other.

One son of this couple had problems and eventually had to go to court for a small crime. His parents learned that if they did anything right with him it was to make him consistently face the consequences of his actions. Prayer was their mainstay through it all.

"And they that know thy name will put their trust in thee: for thou Lord, hast not forsaken them that seek thee" (Psalm 9:10). This scripture was the theme of a recent women's conference and describes our feelings about the challenges we have had as a couple with marriage and parenting experiences. We have had our difficulties rearing children like everyone else. A little love and a lot of patience have gone a long way to get to the faith and belief that ultimately everything works out in the Lord's way.

One son, since age two, was always in trouble. He would flail at his siblings just to get something going. He always wanted to have everyone agitated as much as possible. At age eight, as his parents, we decided he needed to have a concrete example of what his life would be like if he didn't tell the truth. So his father took him to the Utah Prison, and they allowed him to go into medium security for a short visit. Later on, as a teenager, he had several run-ins with the law.

One evening about 10 PM he was accompanied home by the sheriff, who said he was in trouble. The sheriff wanted to read him his rights before questioning him. I answered, "We don't need that. Just tell us what happened." He related that a fellow had a minor accident along the road. When the man walked to the nearest house for help, our son and his buddy tried to steal some tapes from his car. The man and his son saw our son and his buddy and came running with fists flying. The man succeeded in hitting our son several times in the face. Speaking as his father, I told our son I was glad he was caught in the act, sorry that he was hurt, but grateful he was learning the consequences of breaking the law.

Later my son and I went to see the judge together, and he had to pay a fine that we made him work to earn. If we did anything right with him, it was to consistently help him face the consequences of his actions. He went on to serve a successful mission and has since returned and married in the temple. We are grateful for his progress, but our knees were nearly worn out in prayer for him.

This mother in searching for a new husband felt through prayer that she would find him through the eyes of her children.

When I was searching for a husband I went to the Lord in prayer and gave him a list of attributes that I felt were important in a husband, father, and friend. When I was searching for work, I was hired by a title company. I didn't even know what a title company did until I went to work there. Here is where I met my future husband. I didn't feel I had a chance of him being interested in me. I was older, and he had been on a mission and had been a member all his life.

One day he asked me out. We went places or just hung out with my children. My youngest boy was nine years old and the other eleven. My daughter was fifteen. My two boys took to him right away because he would play games and throw a ball around. My daughter was more reticent but soon warmed up because of the respect she had for him. When we were talking about marriage, I sought guidance from Heavenly Father because I didn't trust my own judgment. I had been in an abusive situation with my first husband and was trying to be careful not to have that happen again. I prayed in the temple and the answer came with the words, "You will find the answers to your prayers in the eyes of your children." I already had my answer. I knew I loved my friend and felt comfortable around him. He has a very warm spirit. I liked being around him and know how he will act in any situation. I trust him with my feelings, knowing he won't hurt them. We were soon married. Our love and respect grows deeper with the passing of the years.

.❀. ✿ *. ❀.*

When her husband lost his job for two years, this wife's nursing skills were needed to provide for the family. They became more grateful, humble, and more in tune with their Heavenly Father because of this experience.

I grew up listening over and over again to the counsel of my father on the importance of an education. I made decisions early in life as to the direction that my career would follow. I worked hard in school and graduated from college at age nineteen as a registered nurse. Nursing has been a wonderful career for me. It has given me great flexibility in choosing where to work and how much I worked.

Prior to my marriage at twenty-five years of age, I worked full time. I continued to work full time for about a year after I was married. As children came, I worked less and less, until I was only helping out at a doctor's office a few days every month. Then life threw in some added challenges.

My stepson, who lived with us full time, started having many complex problems. Even with the help of counselors, we were unable to keep peace in our home and provide him with the help that he needed. We opted to enroll him at Utah Boys Ranch. This helped with the peace within our home with the other children, but added increased emotional and financial stress to our marriage. Organizations such as the Boys Ranch are very expensive. I knew that I needed to help with the bills. My husband never asked me to go back to work. He felt strongly that he should be the breadwinner and couldn't impose that responsibility upon me.

I watched as our savings continued to dwindle. For about six months I knew that I needed to go back to work but dreaded leaving my family to do it. Finally, I went back to the hospital unit that I had been working for before and was welcomed with open arms. I worked part-time, just enough to make up the difference that we needed to pay for our son's bills. I was grateful for a husband who felt within himself a strong sense of responsibility in his role of provider for our family. He didn't make it a requirement that I work as well to increase our standard of living. Knowing of his integrity made it easier for me to make the decision on my own.

When our son was about a year into his treatment program that would eventually last for another year, my husband came home early from work one day with news that sent our entire family, especially him, reeling. He had lost his job! We found comfort in the love that we had for each other and most especially in the love of our Father in Heaven. We prayed more earnestly every day. How were we going to make it through this crisis? The obvious answer was for me to start working more. I had to be the breadwinner, and I knew that I had to do it without complaint. In my husband's eyes, he had failed at one of the basic duties given to him in caring for our family. This was going to be a very difficult time for him. I couldn't make it worse by making him feel like he wasn't pulling his weight.

I chose to work twelve-hour and sixteen-hour night shifts. I didn't make as much as he did and so had to work more hours. I worked on average, sixty hours a week. This kept us afloat, but still wasn't the income that we were accustomed to. Working nights allowed me to have a few hours each day with the children. I did as much of the routine activities with them as I could.

My husband became Mr. Mom. He carpooled, cleaned house, helped with homework, learned more patience, put kids to bed, and so forth. During the beginning of this seemingly unending ordeal, we ended up having three of our nephews live with us for four months. At the ages of one, three, and five, they certainly added to the mounting concerns in our home.

During all of this, my husband had a new job, which was to find a job. He tried to spend eight hours a day doing this. We had humbled ourselves and had analyzed our lifestyle. We had figured that he could accept employment at a salary that was just sixty percent of his previous income and could manage our family at that level, although not without discomfort. Weeks of hoping for the right job to come along turned to months of discouragement. Months of discouragement turned to lowered feelings of self-worth and feelings of inadequacy.

The one year mark came and went, then the eighteen-month mark passed, and still no job. My New Year's resolution for the previous year was "No Whining." It proved to be a worthwhile goal. I learned to be cheerful and supportive despite all the challenges. I knew that even though this was tough on me physically, to work all night, get four to five hours of sleep and try to be cheerful for my family when they came home from school, it was tremendously more difficult for my husband to go day after day, with literally thousands of resumes submitted, and still be upbeat and feel worthwhile.

Our family learned to be grateful for what we had. We learned to see the good in all that was around us. The children were careful in deciding what they asked for. We learned to put our trust in the Lord and saw His hand in everything around us. We learned to say 'Thy will be done' and got to the point of saying "please help us learn what it is that we are to learn so that we can be better servants and help those around us."

Exactly one week short of two years from the day that my husband lost his job, he was given an amazing job offer! It was a better position than the job he had before. It was at a higher income than he had before, and it was with a very secure company. He has since advanced within the company. We count our blessings every day. Even now more than a year after his employment, the children still remember (without encouragement) to be thankful that Dad has a job.

I have returned to working the bare minimum to keep my license current, and I get to sleep at night. The experience was one that brought us closer together as a family. My husband and I loved each other more deeply and cared more deeply for our children and their struggles. We came to understand each other more. We felt the Spirit in greater abundance in our home. It is something that I would never have asked for, but I am grateful for what it has taught us.

2

Make Decisions Early

Wouldn't it be wonderful to be able to enjoy the peace and comfort afforded those who plan ahead for the important events and experiences in their lives?

This couple never used credit cards and have borrowed money only for their car and home. They have faithfully followed their goals. Their children learned responsibility early and thank their parents for it.

When my wife and I married, even before our children came to us, we sat down and set some realistic goals. I have never been a wage earner with a great income. We planned together. Priorities were set first that we could complete. For instance, we never used a credit card nor borrowed money except for our car and payments for our home. We saved religiously for the things that would benefit our home. We went without a lot of things at first, but our situation improved year by year.

We taught our children to have responsibility during their formative years. We wanted them to know that if our bedroom was kept in order, theirs should be also. We taught them the value of money and what it could and could not do. Each child had a savings account with my wife. We encouraged them to pay their tithing when we did. When the Jordan River Temple was under construction, we decided together to each make a sizeable contribution.

In their junior and senior high school years, our children felt that we were too strict towards them because many of the parents of their friends were affluent. We could do things for them in a financial way, such as paying for college and other expenses, but each child worked hard at chores they didn't like. Many years later they each told us how much they loved us for teaching them responsibility.

We had rough times along with the good, but the Lord showed us the way. We followed good, sound principles. We always made our children feel important, no matter the crisis, and taught them to forgive and forget. Each child has established a home of love and religious practices. We hold our breath at times, realizing that Satan is real. Through our wrongdoing, we give him power that ultimately can destroy us. Together we all share the hurdles, joys, and successes.

Our children never got away with anything that was wrong. We have tried to love them into understanding what is right and wrong, and in being honest and responsible. My wife and I have never physically abused our children although at times I felt like placing a hand on them. They were more hurt when we were disappointed in them. It is good to look back on our children and see how they have managed themselves. We have had a happy, successful marriage through planning ahead before we even had children.

Through this bishop's experiences he has learned that being unselfish is the most important character trait one can develop. We need to live worthy of the blessings the Lord would like to give us.

My wife and I were married in the Salt Lake Temple on the fourteenth day of February in 1950. Elder Harold B. Lee, who at that time was a member of the Twelve Apostles, performed the marriage ceremony for us. He really impressed me with the things he said. I have used the instructions he gave us many times over the years in talking to young people and in performing weddings as a bishop and later in the temple as a sealer. I won't tell you all that he said, but I would like to relate this one part.

He came over to where we were seated and stood right in front of us. His knee was next to mine. He looked down at me and tapped me on the knee and said, "Look at your wife-to-be. Isn't she beautiful?" I turned and looked at her. She was so very beautiful, and I loved her so much. He said, "She couldn't do anything wrong, could she?" I looked at Elder Lee, and said "Oh, no!" He then took his finger and put it next to my nose, and while moving it up and down to make a point, he said, "Remember that, remember that, remember that." He then turned to my wife-to-be and did the same thing. He asked her to look at me. Then he said, "Isn't he handsome!" She nodded in agreement. He then said, "He couldn't do anything wrong, could he?" She said, "No," just as I had. Then Elder Lee said the same thing to her, "Remember that, remember that, remember that."

He then went on to explain that before marriage you really need to be critical, make sure that your mate has all the qualities that you have been looking for. Then after marriage, you put on blinders and see only the good things in each other for the rest of your lives. That was such good advice. It has really helped our marriage to run much more smoothly, like the Lord would want it to.

He also told us the importance of praying together and never going to bed with a problem between us unresolved. He told us the importance of paying our tithing, being morally clean, and being worthy to receive the blessings the Lord would like to give us. It was wonderful, and I have never forgotten his instruction.

A few years later Elder Lee became President of the Church. Having been a bishop three different times in my life and having served as a mission president, working with several hundred young missionaries, I have had many opportunities to counsel people and work with them on their marriage problems. Now I am much older, and as I look back on my life and the lives of my children and friends, one thing strikes me as the very most important character trait a person needs to cultivate and work at daily. That is the art of unselfishness.

Almost without exception, when a couple is having marriage problems, either one or both of them are looking inward and feeling sorry for themselves, thinking only of what their partner needs to change to make the marriage work, rather than trying to find what they can change in themselves to make life better for their partner and their family.

The Savior told us many times in the scriptures that we need to lose ourselves in the service of others. The more we serve others and forget about what we want, the more we find happiness and joy. Every couple I know that has found joy and happiness in their marriage has learned to give of themselves, sacrificing of their own time and wants.

The Savior gave us a perfect example of complete unselfishness. He even went so far as to give his life for all of us. I can say without any hesitation that if each person will truly put his partner's needs and wants ahead of his own, he cannot help but be successful, and have the joy and happiness we all seek. If you allow yourself to be selfish and become angry or unkind with your partner or others, you are opening the door to unhappiness. But if each person remembers the importance of being unselfish and recaptures the beauty of your marriage each morning, all you will see is the fulness of joy and happiness that is there to be enjoyed. I truly know this to be true!

This wife learned to think of the good things about her husband in order to stay together. This helped him to know he was the most important person in her life. A husband and wife need to come to an agreement on what in their lives has priority.

I grew up in a home that was very organized while my husband grew up in a less than organized household. I could barely abide the mess that he thought was fine. In order for us to stay together, I had to let go of some things and think of the good about my husband. This helped him know that he was the most important and also gave him an idea by observing me of how I would like things to be. He also changed to a degree.

We decided that our family and ourselves were more important than trying to have a tidy home. This has worked for many years. We have seven boys and have just the youngest to send on a mission, so we feel we have had a successful marriage.

This husband and wife are very different in many ways. They decided to make their differences work for them instead of against them. They have developed similar interests and have become best friends.

During the first few years of marriage, when we had disagreements, we realized that our ideas of how things should be done were quite different from each other. I was very forceful and felt my plans and ideas were right.

On the other hand, my husband was patient and loving and said we should think the situation over for a couple of days and then talk about it again to decide on the best solution. Nearly every time I agreed with him, not from pressure but because I came to realize that his way was the best. In many instances had we used my way, things would not have been the best for our family.

My husband and I are about as different as two people can get. We decided early on to let our differences work for us instead of against us. Our differences made us a better whole. We both have developed similar interests. My husband has taken me on a date almost every weekend since we were married. Through this we have become best friends. Since our children have left home, we have now discovered similar activities we like that we didn't know about before, such as going to the theater and traveling.

This husband and father reminds himself often that trust is what marriage is all about. He changed career choices three times to have better family relationships. He chose to be unselfish. Compatibility is essential. This couple learned to recognize troublesome symptoms and then take action to make things better.

I think the greatest part of a good marriage is being compatible. It must start before marriage in understanding yourself and your potential mate. My wife and I have many common interests and goals that have made our marriage work. We both put church service up front along with raising a family. It is not something that just happens, either. There is a constant battle in balancing the important things in life with the selfish things. When something does go wrong, it can usually be blamed on that trait—selfishness.

Too many people today seem to live only for the moment and don't have plans for the future. I think that is one thing that helps Latter-Day Saint marriages work better. Certainly all don't work out, but better percentages do seem to make it to the end.

Our eternal perspective on marriage compels us to find that compatible mate that I spoke of earlier, and we keep that perspective in mind through temple attendance and through raising and being with our family. I am amazed sometimes when I go to a store and hear a couple arguing about some silly little thing in public. Not that we never have disagreements, but to hear people tear each other down in public is very sad. I guess our culture today teaches us to always be right and to stick up for ourselves. This doesn't work in marriage. There are times when you may need to argue, but arguing over every little simple thing will eventually wear the other person down and cause the marriage to fail.

I have heard stories about marriages breaking up over petty things, like how we squeeze the toothpaste tube and I sometimes find myself actually getting upset over things like that. So, I constantly have to remind myself of what marriage is all about. I have left at least three careers because there were contentions within the marriage due to work schedules, and so forth.

The first job I had out of college was as a pilot trainee in the Air Force. I soon found that juggling time at home with what was expected of me in learning to fly was leading me down a path I didn't want to travel. Not all of the blame for leaving the Air Force in the middle of pilot training can go to troubles at home, but with taking care of a new baby and a marriage of just over a year, I decided to make a career change nonetheless. I can honestly say that every time I made a career change things worked out for the better. And I always discussed things with my wife before making the final change. I believe a selfish attitude and following what I wanted to do would have driven a deeper wedge in our marriage.

The key to making it through these career changes was recognizing the symptoms and taking the action to make things better. This was done through prayer and dialogue. Our marriage works better today because we worked through these things at the beginning of our marriage.

When I was ordered to active duty in the Air Force after 9/11, there was nothing I had to worry about with my marriage. It was not easy being away, but we knew where we stood with each other and never had to worry about our marriage. Trust is one of the greatest things for a good marriage. Trust means you never have to worry about how money is spent or how children are taught, or things like fidelity.

This couple decided to handle differences the way they felt the Savior would handle them.

The basic understanding that has kept our marriage out of trouble is so simple, but is also 100 percent effective. It is guaranteed to work. We agreed together that we wouldn't say anything that would hurt each other. This is to be applied in three dimensions. One is in the presence of one spouse when someone else is there. The second is with our friends when the other spouse is not around. The third is simply in the thoughts of our minds—even in our thoughts we know we should never think things that would hurt each other.

We will soon have been married forty-nine years and have not had a single quarrel. Nor have we had a verbal confrontation. The statement of sociologists to "Get it out in the open," is not the way the Savior would handle differences. There is another thought that might be of value. "Just because it might be true, is no reason that it has to be said."

.❁. ✿ *. ❁.*

This wife believes in doing the simple things, like going on a date often, to keep her marriage alive and well.

My husband and I decided before we were married that we'd had such a good time on our dates that we would continue to have them once a week after marriage. This has been a wonderful night to look forward to and has enriched our lives by keeping our marriage strong and happy.

Often we would simply go for a walk together, holding hands and talking about the things that were important to us. Sometimes it involved going to the grocery store together, or to the library for books for the children and ourselves to read. Sometimes we would just go for an ice cream cone at a stand around the corner and bring home ice cream for the family to enjoy as well.

.❁. ✿ *. ❁.*

Don't hold a grudge. This can affect you forever. If you cannot change a situation, it is best to let it go.

My husband and I found out early in our marriage that we did not want to hold grudges. We decided that once a situation was over, we couldn't do anything to change it, so it was best to let it go. This was why I disliked ironing. Where we lived our radio didn't work during the day. While I ironed I used to go over and over something that had bothered me. Then I started having one of my children read to me as I ironed. This helped me a lot to abide by our decision to not hold a grudge.

.❁. ✿ *. ❁.*

This husband knew that giving his children a legacy of stability and moral values by the way he and his wife treated one another would help his children create their own eternal families.

When my fiancée and I were first in the process of making arrangements for our big day, we met with our stake president. He gave us some advice and counsel that I have since come to find very valuable.

I was twenty-four and maybe just a little rebellious yet, but determined to get off on the right track. He told us to avoid watching R-rated movies at any time. There are so many ideas and pictures that fill your head in everyday life and that are involuntary, that it makes sense to screen out some of the negative and corrupting influences that we can control.

Certainly our entertainment falls into this category. We as adults sometimes feel as though we are mature and can handle anything. After all, it's just entertainment.

When I first build a decorative pond, it is so pristine and beautiful, but once the sediment has slowly built up to about one inch deep, it starts to emit a very foul odor. That one inch of silt is all it takes to support other microorganisms that cause the stench. This process is very gradual, but in a pond, it can be easily fixed.

The images and thoughts in our minds are not so easy to erase. In fact it sometimes seems impossible to erase them. This slow but steady degradation of thinking, over time, can influence our relationships with others, with God, and with ourselves.

I have found in my marriage that setting certain guidelines or perimeters early on, that we could both agree on, has brought harmony into our home and our relationship. It is so important to share morals that harbor respect and decency toward each other. We have made a conscious effort to give our children a legacy of stability by the way we treat each other and by our promise that we can be a forever family.

As my wife and I have tried to incorporate into our new family this idea of modesty in what we view, it just seemed to naturally influence the way we would teach our children to dress. My wife has encouraged all our children to wear the same style of clothing now as would be appropriate after they had been through the temple. When they were young it was easy, but now with four teenagers who understand the reasons, it is even nicer to see them make the right choice on their own.

This wife learned that being together with her husband on issues is the best solution to most problems involving their children.

My husband is such a tender-hearted person who avoids all contention of every kind, even to the point of (in my opinion) jeopardizing some situations. We have had a rich, happy married life with his tenderness and concern for me and our family uppermost in his mind. His patience knows no bounds.

Like many other couples, our only real conflict has been over children. We had a couple of children who gave us a lot of grief as they were maturing. I wanted to be firmer and tougher when it came to discipline. I would try to be this way, only to have it undermined by my husband. Over the years I have come to learn that you are what you are. Changes only come after much trial and error. Our only real arguments resulted over this very issue.

Now after years of experience and trying to see the whole picture, which isn't easy sometimes, I have come to the conclusion that patience is a virtue not to be taken lightly. If couples would talk together and decide which way to go and then be together on their decisions, there would be far fewer arguments and much greater success. Being together on issues, no matter which way you choose to deal with them, is by far the best solution to most problems. We all want it our way, but we need to look for what will work best. There is a lot of give and take in everything that is worthwhile.

❊. ❁ *.❊*

This couple realized that even with the rigorous schedule of medical school, they could have one day a week totally for the family. Those days helped both of them get through trying times.

In the six and a half years my husband and I have been married, he has been in school for all but the last six months. It has been a long road with many sacrifices on both our parts.

Because I felt so strongly about my husband's success in school—in part because it would determine our future—I did my best to do most of the work at home and with the kids so he could focus on school. This of course became very stressful as I felt at times like a single mother trying to do it all on my own. Because of the rigorous demands of medical school, my husband studied constantly, and there were times I found myself resentful of the amount of time he put into his studies. I felt neglected. So early on we decided that he would take one whole day of studying off each week and spend it entirely with me and the kids. I can't express how much those days helped both of us get through medical school. We rarely went anywhere or did anything special on those days. It was simply a day for both of us to relax, be together, and focus on each other.

We also made a goal to get out once a month and take a fun day trip or weekend road trip somewhere. These were never anything too tremendous, usually just hiking or sightseeing, but these little jaunts were vital in our marriage. This was a time to reconnect and evaluate where we were. We always had the kids with us, but because they were young, they were usually sleeping. This gave us a chance to really talk. We'd talk about our goals and our dreams, about our children, about us, about school, and about the future. It was our monthly therapy, and it worked. At home we were often distracted; he with his studies, me with the kids. But on our weekends out, we were able to leave the house, the worries, and the school work behind and remember why we wanted to be married, why we loved each other so much, and why we were doing this.

Now that my husband is out of school, I can't say it has gotten any easier. His work schedule is overwhelming, and we've found that we still have to work hard to make time for each other. But I know that if we do, if we keep talking to each other, and keep finding time to be alone, we'll make it another six and a half years easily. But truth be told, we're shooting for sixty!

.❀. ✿ *. ❀.*

This wife and mother was there for her children through all their years of school because she and her husband decided on this even before marriage. They created many memories to last a lifetime.

I was working at the LDS Hospital when I became engaged to marry. I discussed with my fiancé my going back to work after we were married. He said, "No, I am making enough money for the both of us, so I want you home as a family comes along. I want you to be there for the children while I am at work." I said, "Okay." I quit my job at the hospital, and I stayed home, taking care of chores.

Days, weeks, and months turned into years as I stayed home doing what I needed to accomplish. We were blessed with five active children, a great blessing in our lives. As each child entered kindergarten and then progressed all the way up to a senior in high school, I was there. I took part in their days of youth by being a room mother, going to their schools, and helping where I could serve, even going over to have lunch with them on special occasions. This created many memories.

For me, the greatest blessing of all was that every day when each child came home from school, from kindergarten to high school, I was there. The front door would open and I would hear, "Mom, Mom, where are you?" as they went through the house. The children came at different times so as each child told me of his or her important events of the school day, I was there for each one, hearing their joys and sorrows. They usually got a snack and then would skip outdoors and play. What a blessing for me to experience this with each child. In the evening my husband could also share in their joys and sorrows to an extent. His real pleasure came from knowing that we were doing what we had decided to do before we were even married.

Now many years later, my children are all grown up, living in different states with their own lives and work. My husband has since passed away and I am alone, but I have so many wonderful memories to sustain me. Sometimes I will go to a big store and I will hear a child call, "Mom, Mom, where are you?" With tears of gratitude, I remember when my little ones came home from school to tell me their news, because I was there. How could my husband and I not have a wonderful, happy marriage with our priorities as our Heavenly Father would want them?

.⚘. ⚙ *.⚘.*

This husband promised himself that he would not raise his voice to his wife. This made their home a refuge for their children and others who still enjoy the peace they find there.

Even though I can't remember what we were discussing, I can remember the time of day and the exact street and sidewalk where we stood when I made that life changing decision—a decision that would not only affect me for the rest of my life, but would impact the lives of my children and my children's children.

It was about 4:30 PM on a warm afternoon in a town in California. My sweetheart and I weren't in agreement about what we were discussing. For some reason my anger flared and my voice rose. But what came next would impact me more than a swift blow to the jaw. Tears welled up in the eyes of my sweetheart. She looked hurt and offended. I hadn't really said anything offensive, but raising my voice had been enough. I didn't know what to say. All the anger was gone in an instant. The only thing left was my concern for having brought tears to the one I loved so much. I had never felt so helpless. I don't ever recall having felt so ashamed. My shame quickly solidified into a firm resolve—never would I raise my voice to my sweetheart again.

Thirty years later I can look back and see the impact that decision had had on our marital relationship. Equally important to me is how our children have been affected by that decision. Now, as a grandfather, I am able to observe the benefits of that decision in the lives of our grandchildren.

As our family began to grow, I did not raise my voice to my wife. My children observed that. I also would not allow them to yell or scream at each other. By the time they had grown out of their early childhood, loud vocal arguments had all but disappeared. Home was where these young adults came for peace and friendship. They trusted each other's friendship and, to this day, they are the best of friends and would never raise their voices to each other.

A scripture relates to this whole issue and as soon as the children were old enough to consider arguing, we began to rehearse it to them. They got to a point where they knew when it was coming. It was one of the first comments that Christ made to the people when he appeared in the Americas. "He that hath the spirit of contention is not of me, but is of the devil, who is the Father of contention, and he stirreth up the hearts of men to contend with anger, one with another" (3 Nephi 11:29).

My wife and I have seen, and our children have seen, the destructive influence of contention in other homes. We have observed the effect it has on the love, respect, and harmony in our home. All of us feel uncomfortable among people who are contentious, and we enjoy the tranquility we find in our own homes. Our home has always been a refuge and gathering place for not only our children, but many others who have enjoyed the peace they find here.

How grateful I am for the freedom to choose, for an experience early in life that was poignant enough to motivate me to make a right choice, and for the support of a sweet wife who has known all along that contention has no proper place in a family.

3

Make Loving Relationships

Enjoying each others' companionship is above all other considerations. Marriages need to be nurtured so each spouse can keep falling in love all over again.

.❀. ❁ *.❀.*

This husband's unselfishness in teaching his wife to become computer-literate helped strengthen their marriage by giving her the knowledge to go forward and help herself in many situations.

When personal computers first came out, my husband worked in business and had opportunities to learn how they worked. I was primarily a stay-at-home mom and didn't get that opportunity. With the advent of email and for family genealogy research, I wanted to learn how to work a computer. My husband very patiently worked with me and my slow understanding until the day finally arrived that I learned the basics of using a computer at home. I was very grateful for his unselfishness and long-suffering in helping me learn this important life skill.

He also learned how to use the Internet well before me and has patiently taught me its benefits, too. Recently when I wanted to help my brother open his new business in another state, my husband got on the Internet and found me a flight to help support my wish to help my brother.

My husband always wants me to travel with him when he goes out of town on business. I try to do this when I can arrange care for our children in our absence. On our last trip, there was an opportunity to go sailing. My husband knew that I had a great desire to try this. He arranged a date for us to go sailing between his business meetings.

These acts of thoughtfulness in my behalf are greatly appreciated and endear me more to my husband. As I see him doing these things to serve me, it surely strengthens our marriage.

This daughter speaking of her parents, indicates that all the little things they did for each other kept their marriage strong. The word "boring" was not in their vocabulary.

Mom and Dad were happily married. What were their "secrets" for a married relationship that lasted? They spoke well of each other at all times. They may have had habits that bothered, but there was no name calling or putdowns, not ever. Disagreements were discussed in the privacy of their bedroom. There was never any shouting, just time alone to discuss and decide. Once an issue was decided, they supported the decision and supported each other.

They demonstrated love for each other by little gifts or behaviors. Mom would cook Dad's favorite food; Dad would compliment her or pick a wild flower for her.

Mom and Dad had fun together and with their children. We made homemade ice cream, pulled taffy, sang together, had friends over to visit or play games, went on nature walks, and went on fishing trips. We wrote stories or poetry, read, and debated ideas with Dad after supper. We put dry ice into the homemade root beer and learned to bake cookies and breads. We made drawings and paintings, attended different cultural events, played tennis, rode bikes, weeded the flowers, and went to baseball and basketball games. The list of interesting things to do was endless. Add work, school, and community activities and the word "boring" was not in our vocabulary.

Every family handles car trips in a different way, but in our family, when Dad drove, Mom always sat next to him. The four kids took turns sitting in front, or in back, but Mom and Dad always sat together, so she could pat his knee and he could squeeze her arm. These little gestures kept their relationship going. The subtlety wasn't lost on us, or our friends and relatives. Many years later people still comment about always seeing Mom and Dad together and about how they treated each other. In word and deed, they created a long-lasting, wonderful marriage relationship.

.❀. ✿ *.❀.*

This couple decided to have a life after retirement. They bought a home on wheels and have been traveling all over the United States ever since. They enjoy meeting new people and seeing new places very much.

I always dreamed of a perfect marriage, perfect husband, perfect house, perfect children, perfect finances, and so forth. Well, so much for perfection. I ended up divorced after twenty-four years of marriage. I still think my children are perfect and now my grandchildren are, well . . . almost perfect.

Now after twenty years of marriage to an almost-perfect husband, I can see that he has a few faults and I have a few of my own, but we get along very well together. We are enjoying life just being together and doing lots of traveling around the states.

We decided to get a life after retirement, and we did just that. We bought a house on wheels and are now going on eleven years of "RV-ing." Life is grand, and marriage is great. You might think living in a fifth wheel that's only thirty-eight feet long for five or six months out of a year would make us tired and annoyed with each other. No. We are just having the best of times. We spend so much time together enjoying one another's company. While out on the road we do our laundry together. We do our grocery shopping together, take our walks together, and when at home we do our landscaping and yard work together as well.

In all our travels I've never run onto an unhappy camper. When at the laundry room, you always see both husband and wife doing the laundry together—never just one. RV-ing must do something. Everyone seems so happy and friendly. Our marriage has made us best friends, lovers, and companions.

Now, I'm not saying everything is all roses and peaches and cream. Maybe we don't do things the same way. There are worries, mixed priorities, and little time, but we find a way to work those problems out. We do have our ups and downs and heartaches, but there is always another day full of laughter and sunshine. Together we have built a great marriage.

This wife says we should encourage our husbands to use their priesthood to bless and comfort our families. This will bring us closer to each other.

I read one time that a magazine reported the results of a study conducted by a life insurance company wherein it was mentioned that husbands who kissed their wives every morning lived an average of five years longer, earned more money, were ill almost half as often as others, and were involved in fewer automobile accidents.

Also noted was the information that kissing and hugging release endorphins, which give mind and body a sense of genuine well-being that is translated into better health. I decided that a kiss (or more) a day would make a difference, beyond a loving relationship.

In 1 Corinthians 7:3 we read: "Let the husband render unto the wife due benevolence: and likewise also the wife unto the husband."

I have always done this and I feel it helps our relationship. When I think of my spouse during the day, it is always with a kind thought. If we follow the gospel and let our husbands use their priesthood to bless and comfort us, it will also bring us closer to them. This works for us and makes for a much happier marriage.

This couple went through nearly unbelievable trials and joys to have the husband well enough to serve a senior mission with his wife. He has since passed away, but not before he realized his great dream.

My husband of twenty-two years had always wanted to serve a mission. He was not afforded the opportunity because of the Korean War. He served in the Army for two years instead. However, he and a military buddy who had served a mission prior to joining the military, had success doing missionary work while stationed at Fort Ord, California Army base. They decided to read their scriptures together outdoors during breaks where others could see them and perhaps ask what they were reading. It worked! One day an enlisted man asked if he could read the Bible with them. That lead to their introducing the Book of Mormon to him. From this he quickly recognized the truth. He returned to his home in Washington, brought his wife back with him, and they were both baptized.

My husband received much joy and satisfaction at their conversion. Subsequently, several generations have enjoyed the fruits of his labor. But he always felt he had missed out on not being able to serve a full-time mission.

Thirty-plus years later, he and I met and married. The emphasis for senior couples to serve a missions was just beginning. As the years went by, more and more emphasis was placed on couple missions, and he expressed the desire for us to serve. Our goal was to turn in our mission papers as soon as I retired.

We had been married for twenty years when we had a major setback. Early in January 2001, two months before my retirement, my husband underwent a quadruple heart bypass. Because of his diabetes, things did not go too smoothly. He spent forty days in the hospital, mostly in intensive care. He had kidney dialysis several times, and it looked as though he would be required to have it done three times a week after returning home. This would put an end to our mission plans. I remained optimistic and was just grateful that my husband's life had been spared. Our nearby hospital had a dialysis machine, so we knew this situation could be handled just fine.

Because my husband would need constant care once he was released from the hospital, I took my retirement early and set my new-found goal of taking care of my husband and helping him recover as much as possible. A pleasant development showed that his kidneys had begun functioning on their own and that he would not need the dialysis after all!

We settled down to a routine of morning therapy for his heart at the rehabilitation center next to the hospital. After a few weeks, his legs began to hurt and he could no longer endure the exercise walking on the treadmill. He was told to return when he was able to do the exercises required for his therapy. He would spend his time at home in much pain, rubbing his legs and hurting so terribly. The pain became so severe that he could only sleep two hours at a time. We purchased a love seat lounge chair so I could be close to him night and day to rub his legs, read, or watch a movie with him to keep his mind from thinking of the pain.

His legs soon became so weak that he needed to use a walker and gradually a wheelchair. A visit to the neurologist at the University of Utah showed that he had Diabetic Neuropathy. It is not curable but with therapy we learned his situation could be improved somewhat. The neurologist said he could go to the University of Utah's Pain Clinic and see a pain specialist. The waiting time was three months. Luckily, we were able to see a specialist a little sooner. A strong pain medication was prescribed, and it finally began to help relieve the pain, although not completely.

During this time of home confinement, the bishop saw to it that the young priests of our ward brought the sacrament to him each Sunday. I would appraise him of what I had gleaned in church that day and we would read the Sunday School lesson from the manual together. Our home teachers, neighbors, and family were very good about visiting and telephoning to cheer us.

By this time, my husband could no longer walk on his own. He enrolled at the rehabilitation center, beginning with water therapy to learn how to walk again. We attended three times a week. I enrolled in the water exercise program so I could be with him. I lifted the wheelchair in and out of the car and happily pushed him where he needed to go. Even though it was hard on my back, I never let him know it because I was so thrilled that we were seeing progress.

After the morning therapy, we would run errands, buy groceries, or maybe go for lunch. We tried to make the days last as long as possible because the nights were still not free of pain. He was fitted with leg braces, which fit in his shoes and helped give support to his legs.

Our daughter, son-in-law, and their family came to visit from California to spend Thanksgiving with us. We had a huge snowstorm, which made the grandchildren happy, but I knew I would have a big problem pushing the wheelchair through the snow once they left. The family realized the challenge and suggested we move our living quarters downstairs where the wheelchair could be wheeled into the garage and my husband could get into the car from there. We agreed, and the move was made. It proved to be a good move, and we actually enjoyed it.

The bishop of our ward very much wanted the couples under his watch to experience a mission and the blessings and joy derived from it and to heed the counsel of the brethren. His program was to interview each couple and have them set a projected date of when they felt they could serve a mission. Their picture was then taken and framed with the mission date written below. The pictures lined a wall in his office. The bishop was well aware that we had planned a mission prior to my husband's surgery, but when he approached us with the question again, we didn't know how we could possibly set a date. How could we know when he would be ready or if he ever would be able to serve?

On one of our many visits to our family doctor, we mentioned our desire to serve a mission. He said he would not sign the form required from him—that my husband was not well enough for that sort of lifestyle. We felt a little distressed but not discouraged. Together we would continue to do everything possible to get him well again.

In June 2002 we kept one of our six-month appointments with the neurologist at the university and after examining my husband's legs, the neurologist announced that in a year to eighteen months, my husband would be as good as he would ever get. We sat in the car after the appointment and both of us said we knew what we would do. We did our math and projected that eighteen months would be November 2003. We would tell the bishop we would be ready to serve a mission at that time. We would cancel the furniture we had ordered and postpone our plans to redecorate the living room. We felt we desperately needed the Lord's help and were afraid he wouldn't think we were very serious if we were not saving our money.

Our second step was to telephone my husband's niece and have her take some professional photos of us. We proudly gave the bishop a photo with the date November 2003 placed beneath it. He happily hung it on his wall.

Once more we approached the doctor, who reiterated again that he would not sign the form of approval to serve. We spoke with our heart specialist, and he was a little more encouraging. If my husband's health continued to improve, it would be plausible. We never gave up hope. We were persistent and continued the water therapy and physical therapy two to three times a week. Soon my husband was out of the wheelchair and using the walker. He could walk on his own in the house, using the walls for support. We will never forget the day when he took his "first steps" alone while we were in the kitchen. He said, "Look honey! I can walk!" and then walked to my outstretched arms. We both cried.

The neurologist suggested that my husband purchase a walking stick rather than a cane to steady himself. We found one at a sports center and he found that he could soon walk quite well without the walker, using just the stick. We continued to attend the temple once a week. The ordinance workers were very wonderful and helpful with him.

My former boss was called to be a mission president. For several months I intended to bring him and his wife a congratulations card. On July 1, 2003 during a Relief Society presidency meeting, I remarked that today was the first day the new mission president and his wife would be serving in their mission and that I had never sent them a card as I'd intended. The other counselor said it wasn't too late—just do it. As soon as the meeting was over, I went to the store and bought a card, returned home, called the Church for the address, signed the card, and mailed it. I included a note telling them that my husband's health was such that we were planning to serve a mission around November.

A week or two later we received a call from my former boss, asking if we were willing to turn in our mission papers early and come serve in the office with me as his secretary and my husband as finance secretary. The other office couple would be leaving the second week of September. This would mean we would have to leave in the middle of August! This was much sooner than we had planned, but we knew we had very much wanted to serve our mission in an office. I had served as a secretary for twenty-three years, and my husband had his degree in accounting, so it all seemed to fit. We felt that the Lord had directed me to talk about the card to my friend. The fact that I took immediate action in sending it and mentioned that we had plans for a mission, encouraged us to not refuse—this was the opportunity we had been praying for. If we didn't go now when would we have a second chance? We spoke with our bishop, who was pleased with our decision and gave us the papers to fill out.

We had many wonderful experiences while on our mission and our health remains stable. We found out together that our desire to serve a mission became our goal in life and that we could overcome obstacles to do so. Any encouragement and perseverance on my part were worth it all to achieve our goal of serving a mission and having a wonderful marriage as well.

.❀. ✿ *. ❀.*

Unconditional love is often needed to get through a crisis. When one partner needs extra love and concern, give it without any thought of being paid back.

Don't keep score. By this I mean that in every marriage one or the other partner will need extra love and concern and even physical help to get through a particular problem or event. One partner may be called upon to give 100 percent of the love and concern needed to help both partners get through a particular crisis. The other partner may only be able to receive love and help, and it may seem that he or she is not capable of giving much in return. If you keep score during these special times of giving and loving, your marriage will certainly flounder. If you give unconditionally at these special times, at some time down the road—and it may be years later—you will find that unconditional love reciprocated, and you will be able to endure your particular trial.

.❀. ✿ *.❀.*

This couple decided to teach correct principles to their children in the hopes that they would learn to govern themselves righteously. Decide how you intend to discipline your children before you have them.

The discipline of our children was discussed between us before we were even married. My husband was raised in a loving family, but harsh punishment was sometimes used to discipline children. We decided that we would never beat our children. My husband never lifted his hand against his sons.

On one occasion when one of our sons raised his voice to me in protest of something he wanted, my husband intervened with the very strong statement: "You will never again raise your voice to my wife in that manner." It never happened again.

We raised our children by the admonition of the Prophet Joseph Smith when he stated that we must teach them correct principles and let them govern themselves. It has worked very well in our family. Our children are all grown now and have their own families. They treat their families with respect and love. They are well educated and successful in life, and it is our pleasure to see them taking their places in church leadership.

.❀. ✿ *.❀.*

This wife is grateful for her new husband and the balance he brings to their lives. They can handle anything together.

My husband is perfect for me. My life has prepared me for our life together. I've seen enough to know what is important and what is not so important. We can spend hours on end talking. This is very important to me. He seems to know when I need to be listened to and when I need a hug or even a bouquet of flowers. For the first time I feel loved for the woman I am.

He is good with our combined assortment of children too. With seven children between us, we have seen lots of child-related challenges. His gentle strength and helpful suggestions have made life better time and time again. We are learning how to balance the children, jobs, and time together. We both make time for activities together, no matter how hectic our lives may be. It seems there is nothing we can't handle together.

.❀. ❁ *.❀.*

A foreign senior mission helped this couple put away thoughts and worries of home and realize the wonders of service.

"The world is too much with us; late and soon,
Getting and spending, we lay waste our powers:
Little we see in nature that is ours;
We have given our hearts away, a sordid boon!"[1]

These words from William Wordsworth are truer than we may wish to acknowledge in our daily activities and in our relationships with our spouses. Mankind has a great capacity to love and be loved, but too often we push that affection into momentary kisses and a hug now and then, and use our time "getting and spending," "late and soon."

My husband and I were able to break this syndrome, at least for eighteen months, when we accepted a mission call from The Church of Jesus Christ of Latter-Day Saints, to serve in the Russia Far East Vladivostok Mission. What a rewarding experience this was! It greatly enhanced our marriage and our appreciation for one another.

We would walk, hand in hand, down the pot-holed streets of Vladivostok, and help each other dodge the insane Russian traffic as we crossed the streets to the mission office. (At home we rarely walked any distance together and very rarely held hands.)

After our activities of the day, we would often stop at the little corner store to buy a few groceries together, purchase two ice cream bars to enjoy while sitting at the outdoor table under the Coca Cola–emblazoned umbrella, and watch the people and the very old tram-vai trudge up the hill. This refreshed us for the homeward hike up about seventy broken and chipped steps to our apartment house and our abode in the fourth floor that looked out across the fabulous Golden Horn harbor with its battleships, dry docks, ferries, and giant cargo-lifting cranes.

At home in Utah on a typical day, my husband would rush off to the office after giving me a quick peck (even though he had basically retired and could have gone at a more relaxed pace.) Other days he would motor forty miles down to his "gentleman's farm" in a small town to check on his cattle or irrigate the alfalfa and oats. He would come home exhausted and fall into bed.

Meanwhile, I would most likely be heading out to a Utah Symphony Guild officer's meeting or a Daughters of Utah Pioneer's company meeting. Perhaps I would be organizing a party for the Young Women or holding a Relief Society Presidency meeting. And this is not even mentioning the cleaning, decorating and cooking in a large home; the planting and weeding of flower beds, lawns, and a huge vegetable garden—and keeping eight children and their families happy!

All this we set aside for eighteen months. There was no more yard work, no more volunteer and club meetings, no more long drives to the farm, no more worrying about clients' legal problems. It was *glorious*!

In Russia, when we were transferred to the smaller industrial town of Ussuriisk, we met and became close friends with a Russian couple. He was a free-lance taxi driver. She taught English at the Institute of Economics and Business, and invited us to teach American English language, literature, and traditions and culture to her students. So my husband and I worked out lesson plans, trekked to the copy shop innumerable times, and grew to love and be loved by the entire English department faculty and their students.

On one preparation day, the four of us packed a picnic lunch and drove to the Siberian tiger preserve to watch these magnificent animals in their natural habitat. We taught our friends all about sandwiches and a tailgate lunch. Another preparation day saw us driving across the vast Russian countryside to a Russian Orthodox Monastery/Nunnery with its multiple golden onion domes rising in the distance (á la *Doctor Zhivago*). The nun asked if our parents knew that we had joined this strange religious cult of the LDS. We told her we were fifth generation Mormons.

We would never have had these close experiences together at home. We don't just head off for a tailgate picnic here in Utah unless it is an extended family gathering. In Russia every morning at breakfast together we would watch a pair of magpies court each other, hopping and dancing along the sidewalk below our window. Then they cooperated to build a huge nest, at eye level with our fourth floor window—even creating a roof to keep the chilly air from the mother and her eggs. We saved gallon bottles and pails full of water for the times when the water was shut off in our part of the city. We studied together. We learned how to run a computer together. We wrote poems and essays of our experiences together. We grew closer to each other and our love increased. I would highly recommend to any couple to consider serving a mission for the Church. It will in almost all cases bring you closer together in shared time and experiences. Have someone watch out for your assets at home, and leave the world of "getting and spending" behind.

Notes

1. William Wordsworth, "The World Is Too Much with Us," *Poems in Two Volumes* (London: Paternoster-row, 1807), 122.

4

Have Total Commitment

Being totally committed to your spouse can bring nothing but great joy. Yet, having the daily habit of being committed to the development of one's own better self is of equal importance.

.❀. ✿ *.❀.*

A happy, productive marriage can be attributed to work, according to this husband.

The basis for a good marriage consists of friendship, love, kindness, consideration, equality, not being domineering, and fairness in all things. I do not believe that the golden rule, gospel teachings, and following good principles, alone, can be accredited to our successful marriage. In my introspection about the trials, tribulations, and joys of our marriage of forty-nine years, much can be attributed to work. We always worked hard to earn our own living and to earn each other's love and affection. It sometimes took work simply to care and want to be a part of each other's lives, hopes, and desires.

As I have looked back into our past, I feel that many aspects of life were our good fortune. First, the example of our parents gave us guidelines for work, behavior, and kindness, and a rigid set of principles to live by. Health in our lives has made many obstacles easy to overcome. Our families' lives were similar. Our parents were all hardworking lower-middle class people with many aspirations and desires to work to gain the lifestyle they would like—not riches, just comfortable living. We learned through education that we were blessed with very healthy genes, of people with longevity and understanding of work. We knew good food and clean living would give us a better life to live and enjoy.

As I go back to our early beginnings, I recall meeting my wife in the fifth grade. I saw a girl to befriend, help, and talk to about the things we had in common. Our friendship continued through our grade school years, developing in junior high and blossoming in high school. We found that neither of us would ever be interested in anyone else. Our interests, hopes, and plans were parallel. Although I feel this friendship may sound like a storybook romance, it certainly was not. There were a lot of ups and downs, but our caring attitude for each other kept us together as we developed a strong, bonded relationship. Long before high school, our goals were to get an education, to make our goals higher than those of our parents, and because of their wishes and their struggles, we wanted a better, easier life.

Our love and affection were there, but we knew that education must come first, then marriage and family. Since both our families were large, we also wanted a large family. We were planning that type of life in the not-too-distant future, but first things first.

My wife followed the desire of her parents to be educated before marriage with a nursing career. As an RN she could work for a lifetime to help the lives of our children. At this same time I spent four years in the military during the Korean conflict. After that we married. I then began my education to be a pharmacist. We also began our family. Over the many years of working to receive the "better things" in life, we have raised a large family of four sons and three daughters, all of whom are very good people, educated by us and cared for in their many times of need, as we truly believe that "families are forever." We are proud of all of them.

As mentioned before, work helps make a marriage work. My wife and I work hard to make our commitments stay true. Friendship and love are constant companions.

Share truthfulness with each other. Have kindness and consideration. Always share money. None of this "What's yours is yours and mine is mine." Always give more than you wish to receive. I have learned many of these truths through the years and have always tried to practice them. I have come to know my many mistakes and to realize that harsh words are only wedges to drive your mate away. Words of criticism or rejection cannot be retracted and come back to hurt you.

One day in our early years, money was tight and I said, "No, because I earned that money." I knew instantly that the words hurt and could not be retracted. I said I was sorry, but the words had still been said.

Together we learned to be of service to others in our professional capacities and as friends, neighbors, and family members. This is the way to live our lives and teach our families to do the same. We feel that our efforts have been rewarding.

.❁. ✿ *. ❁.*

Loyalty to your spouse is imperative in a happy marriage. Push forward and try to love each other "with all your heart." Try to see yourself as your spouse sees you. Be willing to make realistic changes to improve.

I think that marriage is sacred and that you should feel it is your sacred responsibility to God, your partner, the children, your friends and family, the community, and the Church to find a way to make it work. You pray a lot. You try to change your personality if it needs changing. You try to be kinder and to put yourself in the other person's shoes a little. You get counseling if needed.

You need to read books and keep yourself open to useful ideas. You know that in the heavens parents are not single, and you know you need to be welded to your partner to get to heaven. You know that you've covenanted to be true to your partner, and you can't take that lightly. You know that God forbids flirtations and infatuations with others, so you just put these thoughts out of your mind. You know you need to be loyal to please God, and so you work constantly on being undeviatingly loyal. This commitment helps to have a happier marriage.

Just about the time you think you have the marriage thing figured out, life throws you a curve ball. You argue over money, how to deal with the kids, what to plant in the garden, what color to paint a room, or anything that sows discord. But then you compromise, push forward, and really try to love each other "with all your heart" as the scripture demands. Someday beyond the veil, you trust you'll stand hand in hand before God, and he will accept you both, the two of you as one, and let you enter into his kingdom where that marriage you cultivated on earth and tried with all your heart to heal and preserve, will be blessed with perfect happiness.

.❀. ❁ *. ❀.*

Sometimes we need to turn everything over to Heavenly Father when we have done all we can.

At one time I was somewhat distraught with my husband because I felt he needed to help me more in the home. I had also made myself sick with all kinds of stomach problems worrying about one of our children. I began wondering what I really wanted in a husband, but I couldn't think of anyone I would want besides my own husband. I knew that I had better work things out.

After much fasting and prayer, a scripture in Alma that I memorized came to me. To paraphrase, it admonishes us to put our trust in God and he will deliver us out of our tribulations. At that point I knew I had to turn things over to Heavenly Father when I had done all I could, and then let the rest go, trusting that He would make things right for me and for them in the eternities. This child has turned out to be a wonderful person. I also applied this principle whenever my husband and I had any difficulties.

If things aren't perfect in this life, I know that Heavenly Father will make them right for me in the eternities. As time goes on, I've learned to realize the many wonderful characteristics my husband has. I appreciate him much more than when we were young. As for him, he just always said we were committed to each other in the temple and knew it was his duty to make things work.

This couple lived in difficult circumstances in the summer while attending college in the winter. As their family grew, the implementation of family home evening became a great blessing with wonderful guidance and opportunities for all of them.

When we first married we lived in a tent in American Fork Canyon. To the world today, it would appear a mockery as a home; to us it was a castle. The tent had holes which let in the rain. Pots and pans were employed to catch it on our card table, the bed, the kerosene stove, and the orange crates where we had a change of clothes and meager supplies such as salt, pepper, sugar, flour, and vegetables. To us it was simply a wonderful honeymoon hotel. Our love made up for the little inconveniences.

We found ourselves dependent upon each other for survival. Poor we were, but full of faith that together we could work out any difficulty. We had no car, no money, no close neighbors, family, or friends, but I was employed and willing to work through it all. We even had to bum a ride to go to church out in the valley.

As a park guide, I got lots of exercise each day making the mile and a half hike to the cave. My wife got lots of exercise cleaning our ten foot by twelve foot home, making delicious meals, and then, toward evening, hiking the trail to meet me and strolling arm in arm, down the trail toward home. We had two folding chairs in the tent and often spent time, knee to knee, discussing any trials or challenges we might have encountered. Knee to knee became our "settling of differences" time. You just can't be in that position, looking into each other's eyes and holding hands, without all the little irritations melting away into nothingness. Our restroom was situated across the river and a two-minute walk away so we strolled that route together also. No adversities were too great to solve as long as we were together.

In the fall each year we attended Utah State University. Limited funds again prevented a lot of entertainment or activities costing money, so our recreation consisted of Friday date nights attending the Logan Temple. This stabilizing influence had a profound effect upon us. Being together in that sacred place caused us to commit again and again to fidelity, respect, confidence, and integrity to each other and to the Lord. We believe that by "anticipating potential problems and trials," of which there have been many, beforehand, we have been able through these fifty-eight years together to become more in love, more dedicated to each other, and more committed to the principles of the gospel, the Church, its leaders, and our beloved children.

Speaking of children, we have seven. Each of them is committed to the Church and his or her own companion. It is our opinion that our striving to be proper examples and establishing many, sometimes very strict home rules, has helped them be better prepared to meet life's challenges. Each of them has presented his own difficult times and each child was very different from the others. Times of lying, squabbling, cheating, and various other violations of the rules resulted in restrictions and correction. Difficulties with teachers or administrators in school were reinforced at home. The children's misconduct was never justified or tolerated. We attended school parent-teacher times to keep open lines between school and home.

Family home evenings were great life savers for our family. It seemed that within the week following a particular lesson, a certain situation arose which was resolved by applying the principle learned the Monday evening previously. For example, our daughter was once out on a date following a dance. The young man she was with stopped the car part-way home, took off his tie, and started to unbutton his shirt. Our daughter asked, "What are you doing?"

"Just getting comfortable," the young man responded.

"If you are getting comfortable, I am walking home." And she got out of the car.

"Okay, get in the car, and I will take you home." This he did.

She told us about it and said that the family home evening lesson that week had prepared her in advance to make a correct decision.

My wife always maintained extremely good communication with our children, which helped immensely to resolve problems as they arose. I am grateful I married an angel who loves the Lord and loves the commandments. Because of her great discerning powers the numerous problems and challenges over the years have been identified, dealt with, and resolved to the best of our abilities. Mutual decisions on all major purchases and plans have helped avoid conflicts.

We suppose every household has its share of challenges and difficulties. We certainly have had our share of such things. We have not always been successful in solving them quickly or well, but it seems that time, open communication, and persistence have paid big dividends and at least at this writing, most of the serious problems have come to naught. Our feeling is that carefully considering potential potholes before they happen has helped us greatly, although unforeseen circumstances always raise their ugly heads when least expected. Having the Lord as a companion in marriage, and having total commitment to living his commandments and following the counsel of the prophets, appears to us to be the only safe course through life.

This husband knew he wanted a wife like his mother. When he found her, he never doubted that she was the mate for him. He promised the Lord that he would serve the Lord all his life if he were permitted to marry her. He then felt a peace come over him.

I was raised by wonderful parents, in a home of faith and kindness. Our father never permitted anyone to criticize or find fault with our mother or anything she did regarding food, cleaning, and so forth. If we didn't like the food, we either went hungry or ate it anyway. (I think we had to eat it during the earlier years but were allowed to just not eat as we grew older.) If we needed something from the wash that wasn't clean, we washed it ourselves. If we made a mess in the kitchen, we cleaned it up.

As a young man, I wanted a wife like my mother. When I first introduced my then girlfriend to my mother, she told me that she was the finest girl I had ever brought home. I was first attracted to her by her cute short blonde hair and the impressive handwriting on the name badge she was wearing at the dance, but as we talked and others told me about her, I knew she was far more than an attractive girl with a neat hand. She loved the Lord. Her family loved the Lord and were completely devoted to the Church and service. As we began to fall in love, I remember kneeling at my bedside and making promises to the Lord. I knew she was one of his choice daughters and that he expected her husband to respect her and her divine birthright. I promised him that if he permitted me to marry her, I would do my very best to serve him and her all my life. I remember promising him that I would honor my priesthood, attend the temple with her frequently, and strive to be a good father to our children. In return, I felt a sweet peace come over me that brought me great joy and comfort that the Lord approved of my offering.

As we dated and courted, I never doubted once, nor have I ever since questioned that she is the perfect mate. Never have I questioned my choice of mate. I hope I never compromise my covenants with Heavenly Father and my wife, made both at the side of my bed that night and at the alter of the temple on the morning we were married.

Mutual love and respect center in strong faith and a shared love of Jesus Christ and his Church. Interest in and knowledge of each other's hobbies brings an additional spark into marriage.

Having been born an identical twin, I always had a close companion throughout my childhood and young-adult years. It seemed only natural that a close relationship with my spouse would be a high priority for me in my marriage.

Just as my brother and I had common interests and were involved in many extra-curricular activities, it was easy to become interested in many of the things my wife loved to do. We tried to do as many things as possible together and worked hard to learn about and participate in the things we were each interested in. We played sports, listened to music, had a date night each week, and tried to learn as much as possible about each other's hobbies and interests.

I had never been an avid reader, but my wife's love of books changed all of that. She collected children's books from the time we were married. I soon found myself helping her hunt for that missing volume to complete a set. Her love of and interest in books started to rub off on me, and soon I was searching for books on subjects I was more interested in—the Church and its history. This hobby has become a real passion, and our collection of books and church artifacts has grown over the years. She loves helping me find books and antiques as much as I love helping her.

Another of my hobbies has been collecting and repairing older toy trains. Throughout the years my wife not only supported me in this hobby by attending train shows and bringing the children down to "ooh" and "ah" over the sets, she tried to learn as much about the trains as she could. When we would visit with other toy train collectors, they were amazed at her knowledge and expertise in a hobby where most wives were absent or out shopping while their husbands talked trains.

It is this kind of mutual love and support for each other that has helped us stay close and develop common interests. Our mutual love and respect centers in our strong faith in and love of Jesus Christ and our church. We have supported each other over the years in various callings and responsibilities in the Church, and have learned from and grown with each new calling. My wife is the friend I want to spend time with whenever I am free, and she feels the same way about me. We believe this mutual love, respect, and caring about each other and the interests of each other is the cement that has strengthened our marriage.

This couple was told to never forget the reason they were married in the first place. Along with this, they have a special time each week to be together.

One of the most important factors that has contributed to a committed and eternal marriage for me has been the way it began.

My husband and I were married in the Salt Lake Temple by then Apostle Gordon B. Hinckley. He asked us to look across the altar into one another's eyes and to never forget what we saw. I remember feeling so much love and simple, uncomplicated, peaceful, happy feelings.

As time has gone by and there have been ups and downs, at any worst moment I have stopped to reflect on President Hinckley's advice to never forget the reason we were married in the first place. It has been a very firm foundation and a wonderful reason to press forward.

Another thing that has made our marriage good, better, best, is that we have set aside a day a week for each other. Since my husband often works on the weekends, we have always held Thursdays in reserve for each other. We have tried very hard not to schedule anything during the day that gets in the way of our time together.

When our children were in school, it was a perfect time to be together; we didn't even need to get a babysitter. We can still go to the temple on Thursdays and not worry about time constraints and crowds. We can go to lunch, hike, or do whatever we like for that day.

There is one final thing I want to share, and this is really a tribute to my husband. It is ideal when both partners love unconditionally and are so willing and eager to forgive. My husband has been such a good example of this to me, which has healed a lot of potential trouble spots.

.❀. ✿ *.❀.*

The commitment to have family home evening no matter what led each member of this family to be blessed to believe the gospel and gain a testimony.

At a stake conference many years ago, I heard our stake president say, "If you almost keep a commandment, you almost get a blessing." He went on to say that we need to have family home evening every Monday night no matter what, and no matter how many are in the family. By so doing we would be blessed to have our families believe the gospel and have a testimony. I thought to myself, "I want that. I can do that." I made a vow to myself to have family home evening, and we have, and we know we must continue to do so.

Because of our commitment to obey this counsel, my wife and I have enjoyed having our children stay close to the Church. All are married in the temple and have families of their own. It certainly wasn't easy many times but it became easier and more enjoyable as the children grew in their understanding of why we had family home evening and of our commitment to do so.

How can a couple be angry with one another while kneeling in prayer and holding hands.

Ever since my husband and I heard the wonderful advice to hold hands while having morning and night prayers we have done so. We were told in a special Relief Society Mother's Day program many years ago of this practice and how it could help us to be more aware of each other's needs and of our dependence on the Lord. How could we go to bed angry or upset with one another when we first kneel and hold hands while giving thanks for the many blessings we have received and asking the Lord's blessings to continue for ourselves and our family?

This loving practice has been missed very few times during the years. We have admonished our married children to do this also and do remind them from time to time. When the prayer is over, a nice hug and kiss certainly help as well. If one spouse is away because of his or her occupation, or for any other reason, what a wonderful way to reconnect when returning home. With cell phones, it would even be possible, at times at least, to have a prayer together over the phone.

5

Money Matters

Money matters a great deal in any household. How it is used can make or break a marriage. Wise choices are so important. With the payment of the Lord's share first, many extra unforeseen blessings can be yours.

.❀. ✿ *.❀.*

This wife learned a valuable lesson about her husband's willingness to cooperate and sacrifice. His love and concern changed her feelings regarding their money.

Early in our marriage I became concerned that I did not have money of my own. My husband was very industrious and very careful to make sure that our bills were paid and we were financially solvent. I was alway included in the financial planning, and no obligations or purchases were made without my approval. But instead of appreciating these facts, especially since I did not want to take responsibility for the finances myself, I chafed under the idea that I needed to keep an accurate record of any checks that I made payable.

It occurred to me that I needed some money for which I did not have to account. In my frustration, I approached my husband one day and expressed my desire to have some money of my own. I suggested we each have a certain amount of money on payday that we could use any way we wanted and not have to report it to the other. My husband was thoughtful for a little while and then replied that he did not know that I felt that way. With great kindness and love he said, "You can have it all." Now I am not saying that my plan was a bad one, but I did immediately withdraw it. What I learned that day was far more important than the management of money. The deeper lesson was the willingness to cooperate and sacrifice. I felt loved and I realized that the greater lesson was to love and care for one another.

To be individually responsible for different parts of their expenses worked out for this couple. They maintain a trust that enhances the harmony they enjoy in marriage.

When we were newlyweds years ago, we discovered that managing our time and managing our finances could cause problems in our starry-eyed relationship. Both of us had family nearby requiring cooperative scheduling along with all the other appointments and events that infringe on time management. Also, both of us were working at jobs with regular, reliable, but not very ample, paychecks. Thank goodness we decided to address both needs by doing some regular planning and consulting with each other before they became large, thorny problems.

We agreed to always plan our schedule together, so that as we did our calendaring, we would keep in mind that our own time together would be a major priority. It must have worked too, because we have occasionally had neighbors remark that they have observed how many times we head off somewhere together.

Because our combined income was limited, we needed to spend care-fully. Since our work was related and we both had regular, predictable incomes, we elected to divvy up our expenses. By working this arrange-ment out, we were each expected to pay for those charges, budget items, and expenses that were designated to our own responsibility and we were expected to discharge them in a timely fashion. We also agreed to con-sult each other on how we were spending money, making purchases, and selecting purchases.

Eventually we discovered another hurdle of making sure we each had the checkbook when we were in need of making a payment or purchase. Even though we had already addressed our time management, working it out so each of us had the checkbook at the right time became increasingly complicated as our work changed and our children came along. We finally solved this problem by both of us having our own checking account so we could have separate checkbooks. This is still working even now as we rely more on credit cards, which we pay off monthly to avoid exorbitant and wasteful interest charges, and to continue to operate within our means.

After thirty-five years of marriage, our starry-eyed system still works. We calendar about everything together, at least consulting each other before making time commitments, to keep our schedules agreeable and to have a manageable calendar so we have quality time together.

Although managing our finances has evolved over the years, the basic premise, to be individually responsible for separate parts of our expenses, and to plan expenditures together, particularly shopping for and selecting major purchases, has helped us avoid money problems and maintain a trust, which enhances the harmony we enjoy in our marriage.

This couple felt they both needed to have access to some money for discretionary use. Neither spouse should try to control the other spouse. Each has a right to his or her own opinion, and each has a right to make his or her own choices, but each must also suffer the consequences of those choices.

We found that discussion of the pros and cons of the matter before us led to far better feelings between us, even if we couldn't come to an agreement for a few days. We realized also that I shouldn't control my wife by making her dependent on me for everything she spent. Both of us needed to have access to some money, even though the amount was small, to use as we needed without a complete accounting of it. Anything that would require a large purchase was discussed in detail and thought about carefully by both of us before buying. This worked well in our home and saved us from a lot of impulse buying and the frayed nerves and worries that accompany it.

Paying the regular and emergency bills became the job of this husband. His wife received money for groceries, small clothing, and miscellaneous items. This worked well for them.

My husband was very good with finances. He had to work hard as a child and a teenager to help his family. He went through the Depression so he knew that by hard work, you can earn money. With good common horse sense you can then save that money for other days. He was slow to do a lot of spending, but he was not so careful that we couldn't spend some money for fun or to go out to dinner.

When we found our home in the country years ago, my husband paid cash for the property, which we dearly loved. I didn't learn about it until many years later. We decided that he would pay all the big bills that came into our lives like taxes, heat, water, and doctor and dentist bills. He gave me so much cash every week that I was never resentful or thought I should have a hand in paying the bills. I would buy groceries, occasional small clothing needs, and miscellaneous items. He never expected me to give him an itemized statement of where the money went or how much I spent for any particular item.

I was able to enjoy doing my genealogy work, and we even took a trip to Sweden one year and found some of our family records there. Sometimes an emergency came up, such as the time my two young boys were jumping off the dresser onto the bed, having great fun. They collided in midair, hitting their foreheads together, which resulted in deep gashes. We rushed them to our doctor in town where they both had stitches. They have scars to this day. My husband took care of these emergency money situations, and there were a few in our lives as a family.

Since my husband's passing I have learned to take care of my finances. When the children were gone away and none of them lived close to my home, I decided to sell our property and move to a small town further south. I did dislike selling the land and our home where we had such wonderful memories together, but it seemed like the right thing to do.

Carefully evaluate the spending of money that will benefit the family for years to come. Say "yes" and see what can happen.

Especially when it came to the area of spending money, I was very negative, as we had always needed to be careful of our finances. I would say, "We can't afford it now. Let's wait and check it out later." Then my husband would say, "It is on a good sale." "We need it to finish such and such a project." And "we always seem to get along." I would then have a bad feeling inside and would worry about the expenditure. Often it worked out as he said it would. We did both make good suggestions regarding furniture expenditures and items to plant in our garden and yard.

In our early years of rearing our children, only two times stand out when I balked at expenditures I thought unnecessary, only to find at a much later date, they would have been very valuable to our family for learning and fun times together. Money was scarce in both our families as we grew up, and I was willing to be frugal forever it seems. This can be unhealthy. There is a way to look at money in a new light and realize that spending at times is necessary as long as the amount is relatively small—and it really was in both these cases.

Trying to make amends at a later date doesn't usually work. The time is past for the expenditure to be of real value. Children have grown and other conditions of the family have changed enough that it is simply too late. Life is full of challenges, and based on differences in our upbringing, environment, and the differences between how a male and female think and act, it is a wonder that any of us get along as well as we do.

Of course having goals and plans for now and the future has a great effect on our actions at any given time if we remember who we are and why we are here on this earth. My husband and I do have these eternal goals and are trying to learn more about ourselves and each other as time goes on. We have made great progress and have been successful in many areas. We realize this life is a testing ground for each of us and that we are basically responsible for our own happiness, but can certainly contribute to that of others along the way. When we do this, the interaction also contributes to our own happiness.

This husband and wife are best friends. They decided they would not even consider divorce when times were rough. Different views did not hinder their love and desire to be happy together.

I met my husband when we were both in the Marine Corps. This was twenty-one years ago. I was twenty years old when we were married. When our daughter was, born over a year later, I got out of the military, but my husband stayed in. We soon realized that we had totally different views on how to raise our children and what we wanted in life. Neither of us had been married before so we were brand new at this.

One thing that kept our marriage together was that when we got married, we told each other that it was until the day we died. Divorce was out of the question, and we stuck to that decision. What also made a huge difference was something we had that none of our friends had. We were best friends and are even to this day. We do everything together. We have everything in common. Everywhere we go, we go together—shopping, vacations, fishing, and seeing our friends. We really grew up together as we became adults. We don't separate things. It has never been my money or his money.

Writing goals down in the six areas the Church has suggested, including financial resources, shows that many things we do involve money. This couple found they needed to set yearly, monthly, and weekly goals to achieve success with their finances and other areas of concern.

We have always set goals. We have written them down. Usually the last week of the year we try to go somewhere together and set goals in the six areas that the Church has suggested: spiritual, social, emotional and physical health, financial resources, literacy and education, and home production and storage. I can't say we always reach all the goals, but we set them, and it helps.

After we have set our goals, we look at our yearly goals and set more specific goals for each month. Those goals are always posted on our refrigerator door. Over the years we can look back and see the things we have accomplished because we had goals we were working on.

One goal that we have each month is to go to the temple. We have usually tried to have our own names to do and have involved our children in helping with the baptisms. Now that they are older, it is nice to have them to help do the sealings.

We have tried to have one night each week as our date night. Over the last five years that was especially hard as I worked nights, but we have still tried to have one. Sometimes it might be going grocery shopping or running other errands, but it is something we feel has made a difference. We have also tried to have getaways for just us. We include our children in so many of our vacations, but we also try to get away by ourselves.

Honesty in our marriage is most important. Occasionally we find out that the other isn't perfect, but we love each other despite our faults and shortcomings. We discussed issues in child rearing. We were united on our methods. Our kids now say that they weren't able to play us against each other. We had talked it out already, and they couldn't pull any fast ones. We have been willing to listen to each other's concerns. We have communicated on little things as well as the big things.

My husband travels a lot and sometimes I have been able to meet up with him for part of the trip. This has been fun, and we both get excited and look forward to being reunited. We have a plan, and that plan is for a couple—not just my husband nor just me—it is for *us*. This last year I was told that the company I worked for was closing their Salt Lake center. I could either quit or transfer to another location, which meant either commuting or moving. I knew what our decision would be as soon as I heard the news. It changed our plans, but our family and we as a couple come before anything else. I quit. Making decisions for us, together has made for a very happy marriage.

6

Lighten Up Your Life

Be of one mind, live in peace; and the God of love and peace shall be with you. (2 Corinthians 13:11)

.❀. ✿ *.❀.*

How can a person who believes in tact and diplomacy as a way of settling differences get along with one who grew up in a home of raised voices, ridicule, and negative humor?

My wife came from a good family, but they thrived on inflicting negative jokes and put-downs as methods of humor. They were having fun doing it, so they felt that the receiver of their negative humor was having fun too. When they received it from others in the family, they did not take offense but countered with a put-down of their own. Their family tradition was also to use ridicule as methods of persuasion or discipline. Their most common question for disciplining another person (or for releasing their own tension) was to ask, "Why did you do that?" or "Why didn't you do such and such," or "Why didn't you do what I asked you to do?"

One family psychologist has said, "Never ask why." You should always look for another way—a diplomatic way to obtain the information you want.

Another characteristic of my wife's family was to raise their voices if they became angry, frustrated, or upset during a discussion, or if someone did something wrong.

My family culture was just the opposite. Our rule was: "Do not raise your voice or say or do anything that could be interpreted as criticism or ridicule." We believed in a kind of Murphy's Law: If a statement can be misinterpreted as a put-down or criticism, it will be misinterpreted as a put-down or criticism. In other words, we thrived on and reveled in tact and diplomacy. Also, we came to believe the counsel that there is no such thing as "positive criticism." This clash of cultures inevitably resulted in occasional confrontations and hurt feelings on both sides. I was hurt because I felt I was being criticized or put down. My wife was hurt because I fell silent or objected verbally to her family's way of communicating, having fun, and releasing tension.

Eventually we reached something of a compromise. She tries to reduce the frequency and intensity of her family's more negative approach. She also tries not to raise her voice in anger or frustration. I try not to be so sensitive when it occurs. Most importantly, I've essentially abandoned the old urgent feeling of the need to try to "improve" my mate. If I do feel I have to make a suggestion of some sort, I mildly and diplomatically make a suggestion to the point where I sense that my wife may start to take offense, and then I back off.

No two people will always be in perfect agreement. We have a set of identical twins, as well as other children. Yes, even the twins have their differences. They have the same genetic makeup and have been raised in the same environment, yet they still have different opinions and different likes and dislikes from time to time. So how can we expect a husband and wife who have different genetic make-ups and who were raised in different environments to always have perfect harmony? They can't. They must compromise and sacrifice their own preferences as they negotiate in loving patience and kindness. This has worked to make ours a happy marriage.

Negative remarks bring negative feelings and put the hearer on the defensive nearly every time. Instead, try to inspire confidence with a compliment. If possible work with your spouse towards a common goal.

Most of us do find fault with and criticize our husband and others without even thinking of what we are doing. I found myself doing this very thing and finally realized the adverse consequences of doing so. I did compliment him occasionally and show love and concern but not nearly often enough to erase the effects of the criticism.

In time I realized that adults are just grown-up children with many of the same fragile feelings we have always had. When a negative remark is made, it creates negative feelings and almost always puts the hearer on the defensive. I realized how much better it was to give a compliment on something that I liked and saying such things as, "It looks like you are working hard on that project. Thanks a lot for doing it now; I realize you would rather be doing something else." This inspires confidence and a desire to really work harder and smarter. I find that I can often join in the work in some small way.

Ideas sometimes come to both of us that wouldn't with my criticism hanging over our heads. What a wonderful feeling to know that I can control how I act and respond in a refreshing manner instead of lashing out with criticism. This has really led to a happier man and woman in this marriage.

.⚘. ❀ *.⚘.*

Advice that works like magic is to not criticize. This couple resolved to approach each other with extreme gentleness when there was a challenge that needed to be resolved.

I think that the one thing that has helped our marriage the most was some advice we received from our stake president when he interviewed us before we were married. At that time he told us to not criticize one another. Just plain and simple—do not criticize. We took that advice very literally, and we both resolved not to criticize each other.

This theory worked like magic. If we saw something in the other that we did not like or were concerned about, we held our tongues and took the problem to the Lord. We prayed for our mate and asked the Lord to help us to know how to respond to the other. We expressed faith and belief in each other's ability to overcome weaknesses and also in our desires to do what is right. We talked about our shared desires to purify our lives and seek to grow and become like the Savior. This united effort created feelings of safety, faith, and support for one another, and created a fertile ground for personal growth.

Looking back, I can see that I had several habits that were a concern to my husband, yet he never criticized me. With the new strength I felt from the marriage covenant and the love and support I felt from him, I was quickly able to overcome weaknesses that I had struggled with several times on my own to overcome. Quietly the concerns were gone. The Lord was able to take care of the problems without us having to injure one another's feelings. What a wonderful foundation that gave us for our marriage!

We have tried to continue to follow that advice not to criticize. If the occasion has arisen for which we need to discuss an issue, we try to approach the other with extreme gentleness. It has been such a blessing in our lives. Not everything has been easy or perfect in our married life. We have faced several challenges, but the joy of it has been that we have faced them as a united team, working together to battle the stumbling blocks in our path.

In the Lord's intercessory prayer he said, "That they all may be one; as thou, Father, art in me, and I in thee, that they also may be one in us" (John 17:21). As newlyweds we felt impressed to take this scripture as our goal. We desired to become one—even as the Father and the Son were one—and that together we would strive to become one with them. We came to believe that the husband and wife relationship is a type of that of the Father and the Son, and that there was much to be learned from seeking to emulate their relationship.

Celebrate the joy that comes from giving. Your marriage will be blessed by thinking ahead of how you want to be treated.

Our rules for a good marriage—and we think we have one—are quite simple: Respect one another. Try to fulfill the wishes of your partner, and then you have the joy of giving and the partner gets what she or he needs. Don't criticize but use loving critique. When raising children, never quarrel in front of them. If you have a difference in opinion, talk it over when you are alone.

Always accept the decision of your partner, even if it is wrong in your opinion. Discuss it when you are alone and let the partner who made the decision make the correction, if necessary. Don't be ashamed to apologize to your partner or children when you have been in the wrong.

These are our rules for a happy marriage. I think we have some experience, because we celebrated our golden wedding anniversary last year.

This wife found that she needed to change first in order to help bring about a change in her husband. She needed to be more complimentary about his good points, and show greater love and interest in his concerns and plans.

We all need the joy and happiness that comes through service to others. Women and men were all born of royal lineage as spirit daughters and sons of our Heavenly Father. Having that knowledge should cause us to feel much joy and happiness in our lives. There may be some who are not experiencing those feelings, but I want you to know that I know we are all daughters and sons of God. We all have this in common. Heavenly Father loves all of us. He has given us the opportunity to come to this earth to have experiences—some good and wonderful, some not so good and wonderful. If we are going to be true to that royal lineage, we need to know who we really are so that we can live righteous lives and have integrity and the other attributes we have been counseled to develop. It is a process. It takes time.

We all have our different challenges. When I was a young mother, my husband wasn't active in the church. He was a good provider and a wonderful father to our children. But I was very unhappy. It became like a cancer to me. I wanted him to change, and he didn't do it, at least not right away. And in the process, I learned that you can't change a person to meet your own needs. That change has to come from him.

I learned that it was I who needed to change. I needed to focus on myself and change my attitude towards him: showing more love and affection towards him, not talking negatively about him to anyone, not criticizing him but being more patient and loving. He deserved that from me. I learned to focus more on improving my own self, trying to overcome my own faults and weaknesses, living the gospel more fully, nurturing my children, and being a better wife. Oh, I'm sure I still have a long way to go in the eyes of my Heavenly Father, but this I know for sure—he loves us. He wants us to be happy and to try each day to improve just a little in some area. Perhaps just be willing to help someone in need, whether it be your family, a friend, or a neighbor.

Jesus tells us, and I paraphrase, that "when ye do it unto the least of these, ye have done it unto me." This tells me that our small acts of service are really acts of service for Heavenly Father. Today, I ask myself, "What did I do in serving Him?" Well, tending my two little grandsons while my daughter did some errands—I guess I can count that. How about going with my husband to do some business and then fixing him a good dinner? This certainly helps our marriage to be better. All of these things are small and simple, and yet they help me to reach the potential of trying to become the kind of wife and mother I really want to be here on earth.

Here are two favorite scriptures to help us all: "Trust in the Lord with all thine heart; and lean not unto thine own understanding. In all thy ways acknowledge him, and he shall direct thy paths" (Proverbs 3:5–6). And "let us cheerfully do all things that lie in our power; and then may we stand still, with the utmost assurance, to see the salvation of God, and for his arm to be revealed" (D&C 123:17).

"Let's try it" sounds so much better than *"It won't work."* When a spouse really wants something different from the original suggestion, a concrete, alternative plan should be given for the other spouse to consider.

Sometimes when I did not agree with my husband, he thought I was being critical of him. I felt that this wasn't the correct assessment. I merely viewed my suggestion as one having merit and one that should be considered as well as his. Finally I did realize that often when he made a suggestion, I could usually say, "Well, let's try it" instead of immediately thinking or even verbalizing, "It won't work" or some such remark. For instance, what difference did it really make where the table, chair, or other piece of furniture was placed until we tried it out in a different place? It is amazing what this does, and usually it is a good idea. My negative reply would have caused a temporary rift between us where the other way created a happy feeling.

When you really do want something different from the original suggestion, a concrete, alternate plan should be given for your spouse to think about. This learning and growing in knowledge of personalities has helped our marriage in many ways.

Men and women are not made to endure rage and anger in marriage

from any cause either from within themselves or from others. Patience and tolerance provide the antidote for this great poison of anger, the destroyer of happiness. This husband has a compelling story of what did not work for him, and the way he found what could work for him and for others.

It does take two to make the changes necessary to have a happy marriage. I was married for about thirty years before abandoning the marriage. I gave everything I had financially to my wife and I left. "Everything" included a large house that I continued to make the payments on, along with all the credit card debt. I made the payments for five years until she remarried.

Two years after she married she and her new husband took over all their obligations. I say this to make the point that it is a covenant that a man has to be responsible for the financial things of life, although there may be exceptions. We continue to be friends, and though it was hard for the children, a few years later they are largely at peace and happy for their parents. My responsibility for finances enabled them to get past their anger and continue with their own lives without being destroyed and distracted by the end of their family as they knew it. The cause of our divorce is important to the context. There was not another woman, only the realization that after $200,000 and many years in therapy, I had to conclude that nothing was going to change, and that I did not want to be in these painful circumstances when I was ninety.

Two years later over lunch, my ex-wife said to me, "I didn't like it when you divorced me, but it was the best thing that ever happened to me." So I comforted myself that something good came of it.

The purpose here is to address what makes marriage work. What was it that didn't work to support my marriage? One thing. One thing that had dominated the relationship for about thirty years. It was my inability to master my reaction to my spouse's rage. Her raging came from unconsciously driven associations as well as normal life situations. My reaction to the raging left me damaged at the core and immobilized for two or three days following each eruption. One day when the cause of the rage was particularly unimportant, it became the straw that changed my course in commitment to the marriage.

Men and women are not made to endure anger and rage from any cause either from within themselves or from others. And when that anger is from within what should be the inner sanctum of life, it can be more than we can endure. That was the cause of the demise of my courage and resolve, and the marriage. There were other sources of strain, but they were all endurable. This alone was too much.

There is no justification or need for anger and rage in life, much less in the relationship of marriage. Anger is the great destroyer of happiness in marriages and the hidden impetus to more sin than any other evil, save possibly pride. I believe it a more common perpetrator than lust, which we hear the most about.

So what is the upside that will help make marriages work? It is the dual antidote to the great poison of anger: patience and tolerance. With patience we find our way into the path of compassion and love, which nourish life and give marriage life's greatest blessings. But first there is patience that opens the door to that state.

Taking responsibility for the anger one feels is essential. No one *makes* you angry. It is what you think about what is happening to you that elicits rage. As a man thinks, so is he in his heart, or in his feelings. All the psychotherapy in the world will not take the place of the simple, though sometimes exquisitely difficult, discipline of exchanging rage for patience. You can work through anything if you approach it with patience and a soft voice. But from my experience, it takes two. One can't hold out alone against the pain and strain of anger. It can't be the job only of the man or woman suffering under these circumstances.

My present marriage is a largely happy and fortuitous one. I am thankful daily for my wife's kindness and love, patience and tolerance, and for our growth in all ways to continue this happiness.

7

Have a Good Attitude

Walk with gratitude in your hearts, my dear friends. Be thankful for the wonderful blessings which are yours. Be grateful for the tremendous opportunities that you have. Be thankful to your parents. Say thank you to your friends. Say thank you to your teachers. Express appreciation to everyone who does you a favor or assists you in any way. Thank the Lord for His goodness to you. Thank The Almighty for His Beloved Son, Jesus Christ, who has done for you what none other in all this world could do.[1]

..* ❁ *.*.*

In trying to help a couple, this bishop found that he lacked perception of what his spouse and others truly felt, due to their entirely different set of circumstances and experiences. He realized his own ideas were not all that should be considered. His life was changed from then on.

About twenty-five years ago, while I was serving as a bishop in Anchorage, Alaska, I was asked by a young couple who were having marital difficulties to come and help them. We had eight children and had been married for eighteen years at that time. I went to the humble living quarters of this couple to see how I could assist them. Their children were in bed, and we sat around a small kitchen table in their mobile home until the wee hours of the morning as we explored ways to help resolve their marital problems.

I do not remember any of the specific items we discussed, but I do vividly remember how I felt. I left that meeting completely perplexed. Whenever I would try to define a problem or action that was causing or had caused difficulties in their marriage, the wife's perception of what had happened was so different from the husband's perception of what happened that I, as an outsider, will never know what actually happened. I was baffled as to how something could actually occur, or be said, and be perceived so differently by the parties involved. I hope that our meeting helped them in some way to begin to see the other's point of view, and thus be better able to resolve problems.

Until things can be seen from each other's perspective and each person's views have value in the eyes of the other, it is difficult to have lasting happiness in marriage, or in any other interpersonal relationship. This event caused me to ponder why each of us perceive the way we do.

I had been very happy thinking that the way I had been taught or the way I perceived things was obviously the best way. As I observed the reaction of this couple, I could not determine what the best way was, or even what had really happened. I reflected on what causes each of us to believe, think, or react the way we do. I concluded that we are a product of our environment and experiences, including everything that has ever happened to us.

First of all we start out differently because each of us is a unique intelligence, and that intelligence existed before we were born. Then each person has experiences that are unique only to that individual. We have different parents and even our parents act differently at different times in their and our lives. We have different teachers, different friends, and we attend different classes. We read different books and magazines, see different movies or TV shows, have different conversations, go on different outings or vacations, and so on. No two people have the same experiences, even twins. We are the product of all these experiences, and they influence our concept of right and wrong. Our perception is a product of all things recorded in our minds.

It really should not have surprised me that someone else would react differently than I would to a given circumstance, or that each person in this couple had reacted so differently as I tried to help them.

Most important for me, this event caused me to make an assessment of the differences in perception that existed in my own marriage and other interpersonal relationships. I began to try to see why my wife felt or reacted the way she did when I had perceived a situation quite differently. I tried to determine what from her background and experience had caused her to see things the way she did. I tried to see things from her point of view rather than just from my own perspective. I began to treat my children differently if they reacted in a way that was not the way I would have reacted. I began to treat my employees and fellow workers differently as I tried to see things from their perspective.

In short, this experience changed my life and has made our marriage infinitely richer.

.❀. ✿ *.❀.*

Sometimes a husband has a supporting role while his wife works out her feelings by herself. This was a great lesson for this husband who had previously tried to help and cheer her up.

I come from a home where emotion was not often displayed. My parents were both even-tempered. If there was a squabble between my sisters or my mother and one of the girls, I would just walk away as I was not involved.

The woman I married was a very feeling person, an artistic person, with many emotions. We were at opposite ends of the spectrum. When she was upset, had strong feelings, or even cried, I felt it was my responsibility to cheer her up and get her out of feeling as she did.

Finally I realized that I was doing it all wrong. I needed to validate her feelings, listen, be patient, and not be judgmental. I had a supporting role while she worked out her own feelings.

This made an incredible change in our lives. We started appreciating each other more. I needed to accept the fact that men and women are different, with different ways of dealing with feelings. I became supportive, loving, and patient. She appreciated my needs also. She learned that I sometimes needed to go in my study and have some private time by myself. She grew to realize that I was not shutting her out but really needed this time alone to be a better husband.

.❀. ✿ *.❀.*

Long drives to church meetings became a boon to this family in the form of shared thoughts, dreams, and time to iron out problems. These drives became a cause for joy rather than a hardship. Attitude makes all the difference.

For about seven years of our married life, we were in a situation where we lived forty-five miles from a high school and church ward organization. My first survey of the situation was one of despair and of what a hardship we were facing. It was during the teenage years of our two oldest sons and even though there was a school bus to take the boys to school, what would we do about all those extra school and church activities! This was during the days when our church meeting schedule was priesthood and Sunday School on Sunday morning, sacrament meeting in the evening, and Primary and Relief Society during the week. There were so many problems to face.

There was a community church in our little village, which we were invited to join. We graciously declined, knowing our little family needed the spiritual guidance only ward participation could provide. My husband and I made up our minds to make the situation an opportunity rather than a hardship, so the forty-five mile trek began. Each Sunday we tucked our little family of five into our car and were off to priesthood meeting at 9:00 AM. I and the little primary boy would wait in the car and read until 10:00. Then we would join the rest of the family for Sunday School. We then drove home the forty-five mile trip for the afternoon. After dinner we returned for sacrament meeting at 7:00 PM, a total of four hours driving time. On weekdays our primary boy and I would go often to our meetings, taking advantage of the trips to do necessary shopping on those days.

What great experiences we had on those long drives. We really got to know one another. We shared our thoughts, dreams, and events, and even ironed out differences and problems. It really united us as a husband and wife to know this was best for us all, and it turned out to be an eternal blessing and joy, rather than a hardship. Yes, attitude does make all the difference.

Changing expectations made a great difference in this husband's lifestyle. This was of enormous benefit to the entire family.

The wife of one of my sons became increasingly disturbed that he was devoting all of his discretionary time to business concerns and Church assignments, allowing no special time for her and their children. When he finally realized that the problem was a source of major contention, he decided to rearrange his priorities. In his own words,

I decided that Saturdays belonged to my wife. It annoyed me at first, and I was feeling interrupted because my office is in our home, and I had important things to do. She was continually saying, "Will you help me with such and such?" I suddenly decided that she would be in charge of the agenda. That decision was the key: changing my expectations. It made a big difference in my lifestyle. Occasionally you have to change your expectations—and as things turned out, the entire family has been benefited enormously.

Saturdays are now set aside for her needs, with more emphasis, also, on family activities involving each of their five children—rather than waiting for a time that would be more convenient, or perhaps too late.

It is amazing how extremely beneficial all this becomes. Patience, tolerance, understanding, and even forgiveness were derived from his decision. He says it is difficult to describe what an enormous difference this has made in his personal relationship with his wife. The transition must not have been easy, but now he attends all the children's activities where humanly possible, and loves doing this. He and his wife together attend soccer games, tennis tournaments, music and drama functions, and even cross country competitions and greatly enjoy seeing these skills and talents being developed. He used to be "too busy" to attend most of them, but the right decision has helped them be a happily married couple.

.❀. ❁ *.❀.*

Praise needs to be given as well as received in a marriage. Be the first to try this instead of giving criticism.

Even when we have been married several years, we can and must learn new ideas to help our marriages be more successful and happier. I finally realized that my husband needed praise and acknowledgment from me for things he had done, just as much as I did from him. I realized too that it was not easy for him to give praise, and that rather than waiting for something good to be said to me, I could do this rather easily for him.

Before long, some small changes took place and both our hearts have been softened and opened to giving and receiving and recognizing even small and subtle changes in behavior. We have many years to go and expect to get much more out of our marriage than before.

.❀. ❁ *.❀.*

Combining two families into a new marriage can be very traumatic. Only love and patience can win out in bringing peace to such a home. This husband's commitment to the marriage eventually made all the difference in the attitude of the children.

We are a blended family. More than half of our children were married before my husband and I were. Blending families is a very difficult task at best. A mistake we made was moving into my husband's home. I would never, never advise a blending family to do that. Definitely, definitely acquire a house of your own where you can set your standards, rules, and traditions separate from the house and customs of a previous marriage.

When we were first married, my husband's children were very upset with any change I made to the house or house rules, whether they were large or small. The negative dynamics became so severe that at one point the children held a meeting and told their father he had to decide between me and them. They wanted me out. My husband made the choice to quietly defend me and said that the marriage would stand and that the children were welcome to join in unity with him.

Over time he had to defend me on many occasions. My husband is a very soft-spoken individual. He was not demanding; he just stated the facts. That defense made a tremendous difference in our marriage and in our family. The children and I learned he was committed to the success of our marriage. Yes, after several years we are still married. Yes, we still live in the same house. But that house has become *ours*, and *our* family gathers frequently for parties and fun.

This mom decided to do something drastic to have her family realize her need for help and appreciation. Lack of communication proved to be the root of their problems.

I'm sure you've heard of a child running away from home, but have you ever heard of a wife and mother doing that? Well, I did it after a series of very trying circumstances and little incidents, which built up from molehills to a mountain.

When there are ten people in a household, life becomes very hectic at times. It seems there was something going on all the time. Church and school activities, basketball practices and games, dance rehearsals, burning the midnight oil to sew a dress or help a child who had forgotten to write a report nearly brought me to the breaking point. Then there was "Mom, I just have to have this certain notebook for tomorrow, will you drive me up town?" I especially like the one at bedtime, "Mom, I'm supposed to bring a treat to school tomorrow. It's my turn. Here's the note."

Then there's the cooking, cleaning, laundry, adjusting the budget for a new appliance we needed, paying the bills, and grocery shopping. Oh! I forgot the ironing. We had to do it all in those days as there was no polyester. The list went on and on for a couple of weeks. Everyone was too busy doing their own thing to help me very much, including my husband. He was working some overtime but I still kept thinking that he could have found more time to help me, and the children should have known I needed them more than their friends did. I also needed more time for myself. I deserved it. No one understood me. The more I thought about it, the more picked on and sorry for myself I felt. A doctor probably would have said I was depressed.

Well, I decided I needed to do something about it. So early Saturday morning after an almost sleepless night thinking about what to do, I came up with a brilliant idea. I got dressed and set the table for breakfast, all the time worrying that someone was going to wake up and ruin my plan. I was going to run away from home! I left a note saying I was tired of being just a maid, and when they were willing to help me more and show their appreciation more, I would come home.

Well, it didn't work out quite that way. I began to feel guilty and was worrying about the family and how they were doing without me, so when my husband called, I was ready to go home. They all said they were sorry and would help me more. I promised them I would not run away again and hugged each of them tightly. If I hadn't let things build up or if I had called a family conference to talk to my husband and children about my feelings and listen to their thoughts, then we could have worked it out much sooner. If my husband had known my feelings, he could have taken me out on a date or a drive somewhere to give me a break more often.

Lack of communication is the root of many family problems. After expressing my feelings, my husband and I became much closer to each other. We did go on a date fairly often to be alone and to get away from all the challenges for an hour or more. This really helped our marriage.

Concentrate on changing your own behavior and attitudes. You will find

you have less time to complain about your spouse.

The only person you can change is yourself. The only attitude you can improve on is your own. Instead of dwelling on the faults and annoying little things your spouse does, concentrate on the positives traits that attracted you to that person in the first place.

Take a good long look at your own faults and annoying little habits and work to change these habits for the better, even if it's only changing them one at a time. As you work to change your own behavior and attitude, you will find that you feel better about yourself and think less about finding fault with your spouse. If you don't see eye-to-eye with your spouse on some things, then you have to do what you think is right. But at the same time accept your spouse's point of view as worthwhile. Try to come to some compromise that will allow for the difference in your opinions.

Remember that ultimately you are responsible for your own actions, your own attitude, and your own treatment of others. Your ultimate goal should be to feel that you have become the kind of person you would like to be and have helped others along the way.

Instead of asking the Lord for things during prayer, try instead to thank Him and show gratitude for your blessings.

During a period of extreme stress in many areas of my life, I found myself thinking that if my husband would just make some changes in his behavior and attitudes, then many of our problems would be resolved. I prayed every day that he would see the need to change and be able to make the necessary changes.

I found myself becoming more and more discouraged. Then one Sunday a sister made a comment during a Relief Society lesson that changed my outlook. She referred to a woman who had been going through a time of severe hardship in her own life. This woman was counseled to not ask the Lord for anything for a month. She was instead to devote her time in prayer to gratitude for her blessings. I decided to make a similar effort in my own life. Instead of praying for my husband's reformation, I thanked the Lord for at least three of my husband's good traits each day. I also thanked him for my children's good traits and for the things that were going well in my life. The only thing that I asked was that we would be happy.

I really can't say if my external circumstances changed as a result of these prayers. I do know, however, that my attitude towards my husband and my life changed dramatically. I began to see my husband as a wonderful person whom I loved dearly. The problems, which had been almost overwhelming, no longer seemed particularly severe. Most importantly, I became truly happy, and as I became happier so did my husband.

Notes

1. Gordon B. Hinckley "A Prophet's Counsel and Prayer for Youth," *Ensign*, Jan. 2001, 2.

8

Share Thoughts and Feelings

The joy received from being able to share thoughts and feelings openly with loved ones is worth every effort. Sharing is the secret of much of the success in marriage as well as in relationships with family and friends.

.❀. ❁ *.❀.*

This husband realized that it is well worth the effort to give up a dangerous sport to have harmony in the home. He also learned that he and his wife needed to communicate more readily.

When I first met my wonderful wife-to-be, I was an avid hang glider pilot and had started rock climbing. I owned a motorcycle and rode it a lot. While dating, she would ride with me occasionally and even took some hang gliding lessons but wanted nothing to do with climbing. We dated for about one year and then were married. She always supported me with my hang gliding but wasn't too keen on the climbing.

One day I took off early from work and met my friend—my partner in crime, so to speak. He had found a deep hole earlier on the back side of Beaver Mountain and wanted to explore it. I packed up my climbing ropes and other gear and met him for an afternoon of adventure. To make a long story short, we ran into more than expected. We thought we would be home in three or four hours. Before we knew it, after a lot of challenges, the time was 9:00 PM. By the time I called, my wife she had me dead and buried. She saw that my climbing gear was missing. Did I ever have some making up to do!

Some time later, while I was preparing to go climbing again, my wife disappeared. I looked all over the house and finally found her outside crying and very upset. It took awhile to have her tell me what was wrong. Finally she said it was the anniversary of her brother's climbing accident. He and his two climbing buddies had died when rappelling back down from El Capitan in Yosemite National Forest. I felt so worthless to have put her through this kind of worry. At that time I decided to give it up. What I gained from the sport compared to what it took out of her was not worth it. I have never regretted doing this, and we have now been married over twenty years.

Through our experience we learned that we needed to communicate better and get feelings and thoughts out in the open more often. We have tried to do this as we go through other trials and wonderful times as well. I am still the adventuresome type of guy, and some of this has rubbed off onto our two older children who are teenagers. But we keep our enthusiasm for the most part geared toward scouting, basketball, and other activities that keep my dear wife happy with us all. However, she has given in to letting our daughter and son learn to paraglide with me, which is less dangerous than hang gliding.

After receiving counsel several times from a professional marriage counselor, this wife and her husband, the bishop of their ward, came to realize that scheduled time for her and their children made all the difference in the attitude and happiness of them all.

Many years ago my husband was called to be bishop of a ward we loved and had lived in for about ten years. Earlier I had served as Relief Society president, so we had formed many friendships and felt deeply rooted. We were getting settled in a new home with seven children under seventeen. My husband owns his own business and needed to spend many hours there to be able to provide the constant financial support we required. We were both totally committed to his new calling and knew through personal inspiration that it came directly from the Lord.

Some six months into this experience, I saw my spouse magnify his role as an excellent bishop and provider, and sometimes at-home parent.

But as a spouse, I was depressed and felt slightly ignored. I was desperate for the support and concern I had previously enjoyed. Our family home evenings were infrequent and challenging, with me doing most of the preparations. Our former date night experiences were regularly canceled because of bigger needs from ward members. Time commitments at church prevented our family patriarch's participation in many outings or plans. Because he was so careful to keep confidences, I felt left out and lonely, even with seven children. Our problems seemed to grow exponentially as Satan saw the rift and exploited the opportunity any way he could.

Finally, I decided that our marriage was in such trouble that we had to seek counseling. It wouldn't do much good if my husband saved others but lost us. I found a stellar marriage and family counselor through Church Social Services and went by myself, so the counselor would understand my perspective and help me get my husband to get his priorities in balance. Through loving guidance and much listening, this counselor helped me understand the lonely load my spouse carried and the stretch he was making to meet the needs of so many.

We began going together for about three more visits, and I began to put myself in my husband's place. I became empathetic. Soon we came to an agreement. If I could count on six hours a week—one hour for calendar planning on Sunday night, one hour on Monday night for family home evening, and four hours for a date some weekend night, I would not expect any more time from my husband. If he were available any other time, it would be serendipity and a blessing I didn't anticipate.

The counselor was able, with skill and love, to help us serve as a team effectively. While we both changed a little, my thinking had been vastly transformed so that I could be a support instead of a hindrance to my spouse and his very important calling.

This wife feels that wives need to encourage their husbands to get as much education as possible. She can work with him also to enjoy knowing more of the effort he is making to care for their family, and to give help and encouragement at all times.

There is so little time spent in the home these days. If a wife is lucky, she can stay in the home where it is her domain and the challenges are her conquests. The husband is then all alone in the workplace. I believe that it is extremely important for a wife to know her husband's work and to be interested in it. A man spends countless hours with other people who share the same goals, ideas, and opinions that he does for his company's success. A wife should understand these things also. She should be willing to listen, even if the terms he uses are too technical or mean little to her. By doing this, a husband will open up, and a bond that is extended outside of the home will also be made in the home.

Often a man will just want to talk or expel some frustrations. A wife needs to listen carefully and not offer advice when he is just venting. If she feels that she has some wisdom in helping him, she needs to wait until the time is appropriate to do so.

Whenever a husband has the opportunity to attend a work function with his spouse, a wife should do all she can to be there with him. This represents a united front. It is well noticed which wives support their husbands and which do not. A wife should be willing to help with a company function when asked by her husband or a company officer. She then gets the opportunity to know those who work with her husband, and he is able to let the abilities of his wife shine before his coworkers.

Wives, from my own experience, encourage your husband to get as much education as possible. If he is working towards a degree, work with him. Do not be selfish about his time but realize that he is doing it for the both of you. Study with him. If a wife has strengths in areas where the husband lacks them, she should use her knowledge, and help him to do well. Many times a husband will feel that he does not have enough time to finish his education. It is then that a wife can help! She can study with him. She can read the material and answer questions at the end of each chapter. A wife can underline the important things and quiz her husband on them. She may not get the degree, but she will be better informed to support him in his work.

The workforce is filled with women these days. A man should not have to discuss important things with a coworker because a wife is not interested or is unwilling to discuss his day with him. Be his port in the storm. If he calls just to talk for a minute, listen and sympathize. His day will go much better and a happier man will walk through the door that night. Be there for your husband. Be the most important woman in his life both at home and at work! Share with him, and he will share with you.

Making a candlelit dinner for his wife helped this husband pave the way to better understanding on both their parts of his need for his extended family's hobby of hunting and her jealousy of the time he spent away from her.

My husband and I grew up in two different worlds. He came from a family of avid hunters. Hunting was not only a hobby, but a way of life. It was something that they have done as brothers, dads, uncles, and grandpas for as long as my husband can remember.

I, on the other hand, had no first-hand experience with this sport and found it very hard to adjust to being a hunting widow. Because of this difference, we found it hard to find a middle ground. We both tried to compromise and give in a little, but it still caused problems between us. My main problem was the amount of time that he spent hunting as opposed to being home with me. I would often find myself jealous of the time he spent hunting.

On one particular occasion, I was very upset and I was not afraid to let him know that. I was acting very angry and being very childish. My husband tried to cheer me up and get me out of my bad mood, but it wasn't working. That same day, I was at work and my husband went home from work early. This just added fuel to the fire because he did not tell me why he was leaving early. I just assumed it had something to do with hunting and became even more angry.

After work I drove home feeling very sorry for myself and very upset. When I drove into the driveway, my husband's truck was there. Being in the mood I was in, I prepared for battle. As I walked in the door, I was greeted by the smell of something very good cooking. As I got further into the house, I noticed candles burning in their glass holders on the table.

To my indescribable pleasure, my husband had left work early, gone home, cleaned the house, and cooked a wonderful candlelit dinner for me. He told me that he was sorry for not spending as much time with me as he should have. He said he understood why I was upset. This was exactly what I needed to hear. The dinner was great too.

We spent that evening at home together and really enjoyed each other's company. It was a great night. The next day was Saturday. I got up and went hunting with him. This is just a little example of one way that we have learned to compromise on an issue that is important to both of us. I just needed a little more time and for him to understand how I was feeling. He just needed me to be more understanding of something that meant a lot to him so that he could still enjoy hunting and also come home to a wife who was not a total grouch. This has helped us many times over the years to learn to compromise and understand how each other feels.

In this case, lack of communication over who was going to clean and wash the car nearly brought an end to this marriage. Marriages have broken down because of the lack of communication between husband and wife in just such simple situations.

A young couple I knew were seeking help from a marriage counselor. In the conversations that followed, it came out that one of the problems bothering each was the same. In the wife's family, the father was the one who kept the car cleaned and washed. She expected her husband to do the same in their marriage. He was not doing it. This grew into an irritation that just about ruined their marriage. The reason why he was not doing it was because in his family, the wife kept the car clean. He was waiting for his wife to do it, and it also irritated him that she was being negligent in her responsibility.

Once they talked about it, they discovered the unnecessary irritation and worked out the solution by taking turns washing and giving the car a good cleaning. They even did the work together whenever possible and found it to be an enjoyable task. Keeping communications open has helped their marriage.

Calendaring their important activities with their family saved much stress on this couple.

My husband and I found that we needed a plan to safeguard our time together. He was in a position to have to be away from me and our family a great deal of the time because of work and civic obligations. We decided that certain activities with us should be calendared. Then when a conflict arose he could say, "I'm sorry, I can't make it. I have a previous engagement." No explanations would be necessary. He did this because he felt that his family came first. This worked for us.

When something about the other person bothers you, wait twenty-four hours before mentioning it. It may disappear.

When I was a missionary, someone gave me some good advice about getting along with companions. It has worked very well in my relationship with my spouse as well. The advice was: When something bothers you about the other person, wait twenty-four hours before saying anything. A day later almost all "problems" fade into unimportance and, in hindsight, wouldn't have been worth stirring up emotions. A few things will, even after waiting, seem important enough to address, but by waiting a day they can be discussed calmly instead of in the heat of emotion.

I know a lot of people recommend never going to bed angry—but waiting a day has worked well for my husband and I. Trying to talk things out when we are both tired and emotional seldom works well for us. Usually after a night's sleep we can both put it into perspective and realize that whatever was bothering one or the other can be either forgotten or when important, dealt with together. This has helped our marriage greatly.

。 ❀ *。*

The greatest challenge of living together is growing old well together.

When my husband and I first were married, his way of dealing with anger was withdrawal—what you would call the silent treatment. This occurred until I finally convinced him that living together should be based on mutual understanding. We finally realized together that we could only achieve harmony by keeping an open line.

One should always remember "in sickness and in health." Marrying is a blessed thing, but the greatest challenge in living together is growing old well together.

。 ❀ *。*

This wife was concerned about who would rule the home after her husband retired. She was in for a surprise.

I did not look forward to my husband's retirement in the least degree, other than that we might share a mission experience. I did not anticipate any good experiences while we would be home alone with our everyday challenges. I had been the one making major decisions concerning the home and children while he was at work all day, every day, making the

81

living. However, I was in for a major surprise.

On the day of his surprise retirement (we both expected another eighteen months of work for him and me), I said to him, "Look, I am not prepared to hand over the mantle of decision making right yet! I have the upper hand here, and would appreciate it if you would not tell me what I should be doing or not doing concerning our home. I am the homemaker here, not you." I must have taken him by surprise too, because he gladly relinquished that duty to me. However, I was glad when he volunteered to take out the trash or even vacuum the carpets and carry on with his major house remodeling jobs. His days were as full as mine, and we met at each meal to enjoy each other's company. It has worked very well since we came to that agreement.

I had heard of many men just sitting home in their easy chairs, telling their wives when and how far to jump, when to fix the meals, and even what to fix. I wanted none of that, and he has been very obliging. We can say that we have even enjoyed our retirement very much, except for the few times he catches me playing games on the computer! Then I hear how I am wasting my precious time. I can't agree with him more, but I claim that I am stretching my mind!

This older couple now realize that their example means a great deal to their children and grandchildren. They are still here to share love, thoughts, and feelings.

My wife and I, before we were married or even engaged, talked about how we felt regarding having a family. I wanted to have a large family. She had only two sisters but agreed with me. I think each should know how the other feels about this important part of marriage before any commitment is made.

For some couples two or three children are all they can handle and think they want to have. Others love the interaction with brothers and sisters and desire a larger family. Of course sometimes health or financial issues prevent their desires from becoming a reality, but it should definitely be discussed at length.

Whenever a new baby arrived at our home, all the children were very happy about the new arrival. When we were bringing our sixth baby home from the hospital, his three-year-old brother in the next seat behind us started crying. His mother asked what was wrong, and he sobbed, "I want to hold the baby." She said, "Of course you can." He came through the space between the front seats, sat on her lap, and held the baby with her. He beamed with happiness. Of course this was way before seat belts were introduced.

Since we had desired a large family, the acceptance of the other siblings by each other added to our happy marriage. We found that in order to have a happy marriage we needed to have a happy home life. We attended sports events and programs and took the children to practices, musical performances, and parent-teacher conferences. Scouting meetings and courts of honor were very important to our family. We enjoyed gardening together. We've always had a garden except when first living in apartments. We had the children learn about gardening and help out when possible.

We had family home evening although sometimes only sporadically. Sometimes the evenings were very good, sometimes not. We knew we had to get along and keep our covenants. Our children and now grandchildren are our reminders of why we are here, and so we keep trying to share our thoughts and feelings to have the best communication possible. Since many do not live close by it has certainly helped to have email available to most.

.❀. ✿ *.❀.*

Every day tell your spouse "I love you," says this wife of fifty years.

It is good to have a spirit of cooperation in a marriage. I think you also have to have lots of patience. Tell your spouse every day, "I love you." That is something we do. It is important to talk to each other.

Don't even think of divorce. Too many young people today start having trouble and right away they want to give up. They should discuss the problem and work it out in a prayerful, loving way. This will contribute to true happiness in marriage.

.❀. ✿ *.❀.*

If a woman desires to attend musical or other functions and her husband does not care to go, one option is to ask a lady friend to go and all will be happy.

Early in our marriage we realized that I enjoyed attending a few concerts or plays while my husband did not for several reasons. This was a source of contention for some time as I really wanted to attend some functions in the nearby city and would usually have to give up the idea after asking him to go.

Then I realized after talking this over with a friend, that I did have another option. Now when I know of some function that is important to me, I don't keep nagging. I make my own plans and invite a lady friend or family member to attend with me.

Of course this is done with prior approval from my husband as we have always told one another where we were going when leaving the home, even to go to the grocery store or to get gas in the car. I found that my husband was happy to have me go with someone else and wasn't upset since he had made the choice not to go.

Now that I know I can go to a particular function if I really want to, I feel much more at peace, and sometimes I even choose to stay home.

This couple learned that having guests fend for themselves for breakfast gave their family privacy and options not usually afforded to frequent hosts.

My husband has business overnight guests fairly often. Sometimes I had many activities of my own, but I always felt pressured to have a nice breakfast for our guests. Finally I mentioned this feeling to my husband. He agreed wholeheartedly with my plan. I would put cereal bowls, spoons, glasses, boxes of cereal, sugar, and possibly fruit in season on the table the night before. Each of us then could fend for ourselves when we were ready to eat breakfast with no worry on my part in case I had another appointment, needed to take children to school or activities, or just decided to sleep in on a rare occasion. This unity between my husband and myself has made our life much happier.

What makes the difference between a divorce and a happy marriage? This wife feels it is because they are best friends. Through many trials and joyful experiences also, they knew their love and concern for each other would last.

My husband and I dated as high school sweethearts for over four years before we married. We were childless for seven years, which gave us a great deal of time to get to know each other very well before our family expanded. Yet, we have several close friends who dated in high school, but whose marriage did not survive. I would estimate theirs is the same failure rate that prevails for all marriages. I've often wondered what made the difference for ours.

Now I believe it's because we are truly each other's best friend and have spent forty years making that our primary relationship in life. While we have independent interests, we've put a great deal more effort into developing shared interests. We enjoy having good times together. We watch TV together—even coming to enjoy or endure programming that is not our favorite. We work together. We work hard together. We have remodeled a home several times. We're a mean wallpaper team. We have put lots of true sweat-equity into our yard and property. We enjoy having fun and being happy. We don't take too much of life too seriously. We believe in living right and living well. We strengthened our testimonies together.

My husband was ordained an elder after just a few months of marriage. My husband came from a non-member or inactive family. I came from a partially active family. It wasn't long after we adopted our first child (yes, we shared the trials of infertility and adoption together—no blame, no fault, no regrets) that we realized we could no longer sit on the fence with regard to fully-committed activity.

We were sealed as a family after sixteen years of marriage. My husband thrived in Church callings from elder's quorum presidency, a seventy, a counselor in a bishopric. This association has been very meaningful to him. Together and enthusiastically we supported our sons in their activities and academics. We rarely left them to enjoy ourselves alone.

We've had several turning points in our relationship: the commitment to Church activity described above and a scuba diving incident where—for the first time in our relationship—my husband became the vulnerable person and had to rely on me to keep him safe through using my composure to save his life.

When I discovered myself pregnant for only the second time in our marriage, at thirty-eight years of age, we felt it was a blessing based on our temple covenants. Later I hemorrhaged after a miscarriage surgery. It was touch and go, and my husband had to rely on his faith as doctors worked to save my life with four hours of surgery, life-flighted blood of twenty-three units and much drama. It was a turning point for him, allowing him to test his faith and submission. The true blessing was the bonding and faith that accompanied that experience.

We continue to support each other through career travails, unemployment, continued play, death of parents, and so forth. But through it all we trust each other. We enjoy each other's companionship above that of all others. We respect each other. We rarely argue.

We're not perfect. We do disagree, but we work through it through trust, humor, and patience. We have hurt each other, but the hurt has been short-lived. Those events have only strengthened our trust and love.

We have mutual friends who also enjoy solid marriages. We have good role models in our parents. However, all of my husband's siblings are divorced, despite his parents' solid marriage. They have had substance abuse problems. I think early on my husband realized that I wouldn't accept drinking. He respected and loved me enough to depart from his family patterns to choose another way.

We've each sacrificed some things that were at one time important to us—like some lifestyle issues with my husband (social drinking) and my college aspirations. At this point in my life, he would be comfortable with me pursuing that, but our success as partners was more important to me back then than a college degree. *We* was more important than opinions and aspirations.

There is nothing remarkable about our marriage, but I do consider myself one of the most happily married people I know—very blessed and very grateful.

Examples of love and harmony are the best teachers.

How parents act towards each other often affects how their children respond to their own children later in life. When marriage works, a great contributing factor is the expectation of love and harmony experienced in a spouse's own home as he was growing up.

The example of how a husband and wife treat one another is just another proof that a good example is the best teacher. This is what I experienced with my mother and father.

9

Remember the Best Times

Conscientiously store in your memory the good happenings from your life. When challenges come, think of a happy time you had. When you feel good, remember why you feel that way. Remember inspirational happenings and answers to prayer. Then write them down to read later on. Your words will inspire and motivate you and others.

.❀. ❁ *.❀.*

Acts of thoughtfulness by her husband were like cement to this wife's marriage. Even though he is gone now, she remembers what a wonderful loving husband he was.

My husband has been gone for about twenty years. He died from brain cancer. However, he was an especially thoughtful person, and he was a true romantic. He would write endearing poems for Valentine's Day, for my birthday, or for no reason whatsoever, other than to be loving. I probably received more flowers than any wife I knew. His many acts of thoughtfulness, though, were like cement to a marriage. Here are two examples:

Back in the 70s when there was an acute gasoline shortage, it was necessary for me to sit in long automobile lines, sometimes for hours, in order for our station wagon to have fuel.

One winter morning during this time there was a knock at the door—a surprise because no one was expected. Family, neighbors, and friends were otherwise engaged. A uniformed delivery man stood there with a large box from the University of Washington bookstore. We lived in a Seattle suburb during this time. I was flabbergasted. I had not ordered anything and would have refused the delivery if my name had not been part of the address. The box contained, in paperback editions, all of Dorothy Sayers' Peter Wimsey books. I was and am an avid reader. The books, ordered by my husband, were for me to read while I sat in a cold car, sometimes in the rain, waiting to gas up the station wagon.

While we lived in Issaquah, Washington, I was a Relief Society teacher. This was in the days when Relief Society was on a weekday morning, and when the lesson was at least an hour long. I would agonize over my lessons and prepare, prepare, prepare. This time the lesson was on chastity and morality. It was a serious lesson as well as a delicate subject that needed care in presentation. I agonized more than usual on this lesson.

The morning of the lesson I found a private place, actually a closet at the church, and said a private prayer asking for the Spirit to be with me. While I was out of the Relief Society room, the local florist delivered flowers. They were addressed to me and were from my husband. It was a formal arrangement for a table. The flowers were white. Everything in the arrangement was white—symbolic of our eternal love and appropriate for a lesson on chastity. Is it any wonder that our marriage was a success?

What did it feel like to fall in love?

When things get cluttered, stop and write down when you first knew your spouse was the one for you. Think of the connection the two of you had when you were falling in love. I heard this in a presentation many years ago. It has been very helpful to my wife and me.

Take a few minutes and think back to when you first met and started dating your future spouse. Put aside the business and clutter that has filled your life recently, and take a few minutes to think about the things that attracted you to him or her. What was the connection that the two of you had? What did it feel like to fall in love? Remember the time when you first knew that this person was the one for you.

Now imagine yourself on the eve of your wedding. Tomorrow you will be married. Take a pen and piece of paper and write a letter. In the letter describe in detail the key parts of your courtship, the moments that endeared your spouse to you, and a description of the things that caused you to fall in love. Include the time that you knew you were in love and the moment that you knew you would marry this person. Describe the feelings of happiness, love, and joy that you experienced as you prepared for the wedding. Include the picture of success and happiness that you saw in your mind on that day. When you are finished, sign the letter. Now take the letter, put it in an envelope and keep it in a place that is safe.

In the future whenever your marriage becomes too cluttered and too busy, whenever the stresses of life cause you to question the relationship, take a few minutes and find a quiet place where you can sit and contemplate. Take out the letter and read it. If you feel it is appropriate, share the letter with your spouse. This practice has certainly helped our marriage be the success that it is.

.❀. ❁ *.❀.*

What fun to take turns planning your wedding anniversary. Remembering how it was when you first were married can be very exciting.

My husband and I trade off planning our wedding anniversary. It's fun when you know it's your turn next and you have a whole year to be creative and plan for this special occasion. When things get hectic, I can remember the plans I am thinking of and realize that my marriage is very important to me.

.❀. ❁ *.❀.*

Children need to see affection between their mother and father to realize their parents' true feelings.

It is nice to have a night out every week. But I think it's important for your children to see you sit side by side and show affection. A kiss and hug before going to and after returning from work show that you love each other. Kind acts do too. I think it's like paying tithing. I used to put a check in an envelope after the children were in bed. They had no evidence we were paying our tithing. Then I started to give the envelope to one of them to give to the bishop.

If your children don't see affection shown between you and your spouse, they don't realize your true feelings. Our marriage relationship was definitely strengthened by showing this affection rather than just expressing it in private.

This wife is so appreciative of her husband's mother who showed him how to be kind and thoughtful through her own actions.

Whenever my in-laws came to visit, my husband's mother would always bring something for us. We would say, "What can we do for you?" She would reply, "Nothing for me but do something for others and keep it going." She was a very unselfish person, and I loved her dearly. She was very kind and thoughtful and her example in her home helped my husband to be a kind, thoughtful person as well.

Her gifts were home-grown—bottled jam or jelly, fruit, or a pie she had baked. These were not expensive gifts as the world sees them, but gifts of the heart, which were actually priceless.

This wife realized she would soon have been married longer than she was single, and her husband surprised her by remembering. He also treated her like a queen, so she acted more like a queen.

In late May, I realized that shortly after our twentieth anniversary, I would cross the threshold of being married longer than I was single. I talked to my husband about this and then forgot about it. He did not.

The week of our second oldest daughter's eighteenth birthday, he remembered about the "Half and half" day as I had called it. He calculated it out and realized it was the coming Saturday. He wanted the exact time, and even went to the trouble of calling my mother for that information. He made a card and purchased a gift. He surprised me by being so thoughtful on a day on which he didn't have to do anything. This type of love and thoughtfulness really strengthens our marriage.

One thing we agreed upon when we were married has really made a difference. There would be no mention of divorce in our lives. When things get tough, we have to work together to get through that rough spot, but neither of us is threatening the other to "do as we say, or else." Ours is a much more humble, "Let's see what we can do to work this out together" attitude.

My husband has always treated me like a queen; hence, I have acted more like a queen. We try to always build each other up. We have learned that if we can't say anything nice, it is much better to not say anything at all—especially to our friends, neighbors, and coworkers.

.❀. ✿ *.❀.*

Make sure you have common interests so in your older years you will have enjoyment together after your children have left home.

Early in our marriage, we began to realize that we needed to be sure we had some common interests so we could enjoy each other's company after our children left home. I had been working for an insurance company for many years and my wife was a wonderful mother and homemaker. She had all of her many duties in these capacities as well as civic and church interests. I also had some of these interests as well as some sports activities, such as jogging.

We found that we did enjoy going to class reunions, playing scrabble with another couple we knew well, and going for walks together. Going back to our hometown to see our extended families was a highlight in our lives. We enjoy having picnics up a canyon or in a park, and seeing the birds fly about. We enjoy going to the beach and having water activities together. I have Parkinson's Disease and try to maintain as much mobility as possible.

We both enjoyed working with our couples group at church, planning and putting on monthly parties for retarded children. Then in the early 1980s we both became very much involved with sponsoring refugee families from Vietnam, Laos, and, later, Russia. This brought many friendships, much cultural exchange, and an extended effort to help these families (now friends) over many years. That has resulted in such things as the following excerpt from a recent letter from a young Laotian.

> "I am writing to tell you how thankful I am for your helping me through college! I have been leading Young Life at Williamette High School here. I truly believe God has put you in my life to bring me to Christ. Who would have thought I would get to grow up in the U.S. and have sponsors who were Christians?"

Now that our children are married and two live across the United States, we very much enjoy traveling back and forth to visit them for special occasions and just to get together. It is fun to see some of the same rules and activities in effect in their homes as we had. Having common interests has really added to our happy marriage

Even if a marriage has troubles, couples can have companionship with shared memories and activities.

Many marriages have troubles, lots of sadness, and disappointments. Even if a marriage diminishes in quality, couples learn to depend on one another, to have companionship with shared memories. They learn to calm tempers and ill feelings toward one another. Even when working separately in another part of the home or yard, one knows the other is there, and that gives comfort.

My mother gave me some wise advice she had used from time to time. She said, "When you get very unhappy with your spouse, when angry words are spoken and one stamps out, just step back, take a time out and send your memory back to when you were courting and falling in love. Think of all the reasons you married your husband. Concentrate on his good qualities and the good times you have had together. I promise you it will calm you down, soften your heart, and lift your spirits."

My final personal advice is to develop a tough skin. Don't let harsh words and sarcasm get you down. Let them wash off you. Most times, the next day your husband has completely forgotten what he said and why, so you need to do the same. Life is too short to hold slights and hurt feelings. "Don't worry. Be happy!"

This husband's wife used her talents to help the children with their school work. He appreciated this devotion and enjoys her love for him as well.

As I look back over the past thirty some years with my wife, I am very happy that I married her. She is a very talented and loving woman.

I think one of her most remarkable attributes is her unrelenting desire to help our children with their education. Whether it was attending parent-teacher night, helping plan a research paper, or assisting with homework, she was always there. I can remember many times when I went to bed while she was just sitting down with one of our seven children who had delayed an assignment until the night before. Sometimes it was their fault; sometimes it was the teacher's fault.

They began by looking at what they had, or guessing at what was needed. At one point we acquired a set of World Book encyclopedias to help out. When we were dating I didn't think about this. I had no idea how many children we would have. It never occurred to me who would help with the homework. Furthermore, I could not have helped them with trigonometry, calculus, or even algebra. My wife is highly skilled in all areas of math, science, history, English, writing, and music.

Each of our children has a unique personality. Each one needed to be taught in a different way, and they were always at different growing stages. Regardless, she was always able to give them one-on-one attention. Over the years there were thousands of hours of tutoring, much of it done late at night.

It did not end with high school. Most of our children still needed their mother's help until they were able to meet the demands of college on their own. At one time I mentioned this to my neighbor, who had taught school for over twenty years. I asked if he thought my wife might be doing too much for our children. He said that anything she could do would help them. As I contemplated his answer I realized how much I have learned watching others.

While not all mothers are gifted in this way, it is to my wife's credit that she has used her talents in the most important way she could have done. I have been aware of this for over twenty years. It still makes me happy and appreciative when I think about it. This has endeared her to me and made my marriage a happy one, since her concern for our children was first shown in loving concern for me as her husband and friend.

.❀. ❁ *.❀.*

This husband and father tried to always make his home a place of refuge from the world. Harmony in the home is a result of trying to make each other happy.

My wife and I celebrated our fiftieth wedding anniversary a few years ago by enjoying a cruise on the Mexican Riviera with our five married children and their companions. What a wonderful opportunity it was to reflect on our life together and the blessing of having these special children in our home to love and enjoy.

We, ourselves, were born of goodly parents. Mine were married for seventy-two years. We have always been grateful for their great example of togetherness. If there were problems, they solved them. When there were challenges they leaned on each other and strengthened each other until they found a solution.

We were both fortunate to be raised in homes where marriage and family were important. The teachings of our parents and The Church of Jesus Christ of Latter-Day Saints always taught the value of service. We tried to make our home a place of refuge from the world.

As companions we have always made an effort to make each other happy. To do things the way our companion preferred was important. As people live together, we learn the things that please our partner and also the things that irritate them.

Harmony in the home is a result of trying to make each other happy. There are big things and little things that can really make a difference in a relationship. Incidental things, plans, and goals, can be sources of controversy or we can learn to give and take. We have often seen that when couples divorce it is because they have stopped trying to make each other happy or stopped meeting each other's emotional needs.

Contention and discord is the result when we become selfish and put our own needs above those of our companion and family. Having a family is part of the Lord's plan. Many in the world today have not been taught or do not believe this law of God.

We are very grateful that we married young. It has given us more years to be with our five children. We treasure the memories we have made over the years. Dating and dancing, teaching and training our children, camping and attending their activities as we have played and worked together have made a difference in our lives. Kneeling daily in family prayer has helped us to care about each other, to support each other, and has created a strong bond between us. We are the best of friends.

Retirement is wonderful. We are now able to attend the activities, recitals, and ball games of our twenty-four grandchildren, as well as those of our ten great-grandchildren.

We are in the process of writing our personal history, which is filled with memories and events that were made possible because marriage is right and good, and marriage is where our wonderful story began.

Have fun, laughter, and memories with your children. This will carry on with them and their families through generations.

My husband's work took him all over the state. He would take the family car. We could go as a group to exciting towns such as Moab, Blanding, Delta, Vernal, Axtell, and any place with a post-office, homes, and a store. We went to them all. I would prepare a lunch for the trip. Young children are always hungry. We would get out on the main road and everyone was starving, so we had snacks.

My husband needed to go to various places to check on town records. While he was busy, the children and I would play in the parks—ball, tricky bars, slides, and quiet times of reading and resting. I stayed away from stores a lot because everyone wanted something when we went inside. We did go a few times to see what exciting finds there were in a country store.

As we drove we told jokes, sang songs, played ABC games, I Spy, and geography games. There are a lot of memories saved. If the town was big enough, we went to the library. We entered the door, and everyone went in a different direction. We all loved books, and reading was a pleasure. A few towns we visited were blessed to have museums. We all loved those. Each child would find something very interesting to tell the others—about history, rocks, or pioneers, with excitement in their voices and eyes.

If one child was having problems, he would come up in the front seat between my husband and me. Someone would yell, "It's my turn to sit by the window." We got all of these minor details taken care of at the time.

Sometimes we would meet my husband outside the building and we would have a picnic for his lunchtime. At times everyone became so hungry heading home we would stop somewhere and eat. This was always a delight for the children. We had lots of fun and laughter.

Now as I travel the highways and byways of small towns, I see the parks where we stopped to eat, rest, or run around—mostly run. Memories—always memories. How very blessed I am to have all those sweet times to remember.

My family are all grown and live in different states, making memories of their own. They are taking their families to libraries, museums, and parks as my husband and I did many years ago. We also took our children to our church services and they are doing the same. We had a happy marriage and I am very blessed.

This son gives a great personal tribute to his father, now deceased, for how his parents' relationship flourished, which he attributed to his father's treatment of his mother. His father's great example was observed by all.

Dad always taught a laboratory class, never a lecture. I cannot remember ever having a formal father's interview with him. What we learned, we learned by observation and practice at his side, occasionally punctuated with one-line admonitions. As I reflected on these lessons, the list continued to grow almost endlessly.

I first began to appreciate the qualities others admired in my father when I was in my mid-teens. Because of Dad's profession as a civil engineer, our family grew up primarily in construction camps. Among the men who worked with Dad in Davis Dam, Arizona, was a man I regarded as a hero. He was a survivor of the infamous Bataan Death March at the beginning of World War II. Although he would never speak of his experience, we all knew who he was and had some appreciation of what he had endured.

One day I happened to meet him on the sidewalk as he walked past our home when returning from work. When I greeted him, he stopped for a moment and said, "There is something you should know about your dad. At work, we don't always agree with him, but he is the fairest man I have ever known." At that point I recognized that my father had indeed set us a great example of integrity and fairness in all that he did.

Dad and Mom were married in 1931 in the middle of the Great Depression. The construction of Hoover Dam, known as Boulder Dam at that time, was just beginning. Dad had just been transferred to participate in the very earliest stages of that project when he and Mother married.

He drove his bride from Heber City to the July heat of the Nevada deserts in a Model A Ford on roadways that in those days were not even paved. Dad built a tent house for their residence. It was the second one erected in what would become a tent village. Mother has boasted that not many newlyweds are able to move into a home that is fully paid for. Her sense of humor and their love made that tent a palace.

They lived there for a year while the construction camp housing was being built in Boulder City. The phrase, "Use it up. Wear it out. Make it do or do without," might have been coined in New England, but it was certainly alive and well in the Nevada desert during those years of depression and world war.

We learned very early in life the importance of frugality. We were expected to live by the principle: "Earn it before you spend it." I can remember being encouraged to collect discarded soda pop bottles and return them to the store so I could use the deposit refunds to buy my first fishing rod. By the time we boys were eight years old, we were delivering magazines and newspapers. We learned that labor had value. Dad's admonition was, "Hard work never killed anybody."

Dad grew up in a family of three sons and no surviving daughters. He and his brothers were expected to help their mother in the house as well as in the yard. The premature death of his own father left Dad with a major responsibility to care for his mother. His experience and example carried forward into his own family of three sons and no daughters.

All three of us grew up being very familiar with dish pans, dish towels, and dust cloths. There was never any discussion about boys' work versus girls' work. There might have been one exception. Since he was the youngest son in his family, Dad always insisted that changing diapers was outside his range of experience. He repented of that position after the grandchildren came along.

That was one example we were not allowed to follow. When our youngest brother came into the family, the other two of us soon learned to approach diaper changing duty as a team effort. The problem from my viewpoint was that my brother often exercised his seniority by appointing himself team captain and then issuing the task assignments to the junior member of the team. Nevertheless, Dad has devoted his entire adult life to ensuring that Mother has been helped and well cared for.

When my wife and I moved into their home a year ago, Dad's memory and mobility were already pretty far gone, but he would not go to bed at night until he had checked all the doors for Mom's security. I think he refused to leave this life until he was satisfied that his sons had demonstrated their willingness to continue providing that care in his absence.

Mother demonstrated the same level of devotion and concern for Dad. The example she has set for us in caring for Dad throughout his life, but particularly in these recent difficult years has been inspiring. She has insisted on being with Dad in all circumstances.

Dad always recognized the value of education as a career foundation. His own education was cut short by the death of his father, but his sons grew up with the expectation they would go to college. He told us we could pursue any career we wanted, except civil engineering. Having grown up under the influence of Dad's skills with numbers and mechanical details, it is not surprising all three of us chose a field of engineering.

I only received two direct admonitions from Dad concerning education. The first occurred as I was boarding the train to return to school after my first visit home during my freshman year. Dad's perceptive counsel was, "Don't let your books interfere with your education."

The second came as I was ending five years of service in the U.S. Navy and announced to Dad my intention of returning to graduate school. After a pause came his warning: "One of these days you are going to have to get a *real* job!"

Dad and Mother were friends to everyone. They have always had time to reach out with little acts of service and kind encouragement. Their quick and radiant smiles attracted people. In every job and every community they were in they made lasting friendships. Their Christmas card list is a marvel.

Dad and Mother firmly believed that everyone should leave everything they touch better than they found it. Dad was a nearly compulsive fixer. If the car developed a new rattle, he could not rest until he tracked down the source and tightened or removed the cause.

When traveling with one son's family in Europe, Dad adjusted door latches and toilet flushing linkages in all the hotel rooms and guest rooms they visited. He took the same approach with campgrounds and neighbors' snow-covered sidewalks.

He and mother especially lived this attitude in church callings and people's distressed lives. They have left each and every one of us better than they found us. They have had a wonderful marriage.

Dad's mortal adventure is now ended. My brothers and I are profoundly grateful for the example and lessons we have learned from our dad. We will miss being with him for a time, but rejoice in knowing how well he used the years he was with us. We are grateful to know we will be with him again. In the meantime, I believe we all recognize our opportunity and obligation to emulate his great example.

.❀. ✿ *.❀.*

Enjoy your children by doing fun things with them whenever possible. The best thing you can give to your children is for the security of knowing their parents love each other.

I'm not sure my husband and I have figured out what works yet! We did enjoy staying very active while we were dating and as a young couple. Camping out, hiking, fishing and just being outdoors are things that I love! We have struggled with that, or I should say, I have struggled with that, because I really like to be active and busy. When our kids were younger it was difficult, but now that they are all old enough to partici-pate, we really enjoy doing things together as a family. We started snow-skiing a couple of years ago. We found that is something all of us can do together and we have a great time. We also enjoy jet-skiing and going to the beach in the summer.

We have been on some amazing hikes since we have lived here. We have so many beautiful places that are so close. Our favorites are Calf Creek Falls in the Grand Staircase and Sulphur Creek in Capitol Reef National Park. All of these activities help keep us active and close as a family and as a couple.

Something that I think helps a marriage, but we fall short in, is having a weekly date night. It doesn't have to be an expensive thing either. Going to buy groceries together, getting an ice cream cone and eating it at the park on a swing, taking a walk together, or playing a card game after the kids go to bed are all fun things to do together.

I think for our marriage, children have definitely put a strain on it. We love them and wouldn't give them back, but they use ninety-nine and nine tenths of our time and it's hard to focus on just the two of us. I know I have heard it said many times that the best thing you can give your kids is to love your spouse. How true that really is. We know our children know of our love for each other.

.❀. ❁ *. ❀.*

This daughter tells the story of her parents who had a double wedding with friends in another town without any previous planning.

This is an unusual occurrence which I am going to take from my mother and dad's book, in my mother's own words, regarding her mar-riage.

> It wasn't our plan to get married in the neighboring town, but to get married in the temple. Our parents were very happy knowing we were going to the temple. Mama and Papa planned a reception and shower for us. Our hearts made a sudden change though.

On a night early in May 1921, we had gone with another young unmarried couple from our town to a community event in the next town. During the course of the evening we decided to have a double wedding that night. Even though my fiancé and I were both twenty-four years old, we felt a little guilty and reluctant at having pushed up the date of our marriage, and especially for marrying outside the temple, even though we intended strongly for that to be done later.

My parents especially were very strict. Papa was in the bishopric and Mama was president of the Relief Society, so I knew they wouldn't like what we had done. They didn't. We ended up going to the temple three weeks later. Mama and Papa invited my husband's parents up to dinner rather than having a community shower for us as was the custom.

Fortunately, I had a hope chest full of things and we both had jobs, so we were able to buy what we needed. Even though my husband and I had lived in the same town and had gone to the same schools, our courtship didn't really start until he came home from the service.

The evening he arrived, the town was giving a dance to welcome some of the servicemen home. I liked more than anything to dance, and was showing some friends how to do a new one called the Jelly Wobble. I ended up spending most of the dances with him, and from then on he started courting me. We were married about two years later.

My brothers and sisters and I tried to get my mom and dad to show us the Jelly Wobble. Since this must have caused a spark of interest in our dad towards Mother, we reasoned that it must be a really fun dance. For the rest of their lives we tried but we could never get them to show it to us!

Our parents lived a long and happy life in a small town until they were no longer able to care for themselves totally and needed to move closer to where we children were living. What wonderful memories we have of growing up with our mom and dad.

This wife truly appreciated her husband's efforts in taking care of the family when she was pregnant and very ill.

My husband and I were recently blessed with our fifth child. We have three sons, ages nine, seven, and twenty-one months and one daughter, age five. This latest pregnancy was really hard on me. Unfortunately, I experience morning sickness throughout my pregnancies, but this time

I was really tired and I needed to rest quite a lot. Needless to say, my being pregnant is a significant strain on our marriage due to my limited ability to do all that needs to be done. Fortunately, my husband takes on the majority of the housework and care of the children from the time he comes home from work, as well as doing the majority of cooking. With four children and a pregnant wife, this was quite a work load.

One of the qualities my husband has is that he is very unselfish, and he often encouraged me to go to bed while he would take care of the children, cook dinner, and assist the children with homework. I am so grateful that he allowed me time to recover from my illness through rest and relaxation during my pregnancies, and helped me not feel guilty.

Now that our beautiful daughter is born, it all seems worth it. My husband still helps out and actively participates in the children's activities. His active involvement definitively helps our marriage because he insists that we are a partnership and that we both want to be actively involved in raising our family. My husband also understand that at times I need some alone time, and he is willing to watch the children. He sometimes needs this alone time also.

.❀. ❁ *. ❀.*

This wife is very thankful for a husband who insisted she conquer her fears based on a real, possible tragedy. This experience helped her in many instances later in life.

About thirty-five years ago, our ward began making an annual trip to Flaming Gorge for three days. All who usually went planned this as part of their vacation and arranged for that time off work way in advance. We had moved into the ward after this trip and heard a lot about it and the fun and camaraderie involved so we knew we wanted to go the next year.

When it was time the following August, we decided to go and enjoy ourselves. A neighbor suggested that we stay at a cabin by a lake a few miles from the dam, which would make it easier to care for the younger children.

We had just gotten unpacked when someone in charge came and told us to get to the dam quickly as it was just about our turn to go down the river to Little Hole where we would land and be taken back up to the dam again. We gathered our seven children into our van and drove to the meeting place below the dam. There was much excitement with everyone putting on their life jackets and getting paddles and bailing buckets to use in the rafts the ward had owned for quite some time.

Our family was assigned to a large yellow raft. My husband and three teenagers would paddle and steer, and I would hopefully be able to take care of the four younger children.

It wasn't long before we found out that our raft was losing air as well as leaking, so it needed to have water bailed out. While I was helping do this, we hit a giant rock and as we slid off it, our five-year-old son flipped up into the air and out over the water. I frantically grabbed him just in time to keep him from going into the raging water. You can imagine how scared I was. We were holding on the best we could, but there were no handles to hold to along the sides. The other two younger children were holding on for dear life and were also very frightened by then.

It was a wild river this time with rushing white water and deep falls to go over (and our first experience at river running). There was no way we could swim in this condition had we capsized. Actually, it was the best river run many said they had experienced for several years. The water was just right for going over many huge rocks, and the rapids were fast and furious at times, with a few calm times to get oneself back to normal.

A short time later our small two-year-old son was tossed into the air by a sudden switching around of the raft and I again grabbed him just in time. By then my adrenalin was at full tilt, and I vowed loudly that I would never attempt such a thing again. I had never experienced such fear before.

We finally came to a calm spot and our boys paddled over to the shore for us to get out and stretch our legs. Another raft was there also and had a pump which we used to get our raft ready for the remainder of the trip. It was a seven-mile ride and there was really no way for me to walk back to the dam along the sides, especially with two little ones under tow. There was nothing to do but get back in the raft and pray. Now that the raft was pumped full of air again, we continued on without many incidents to make my heart beat as hard as it had been.

When we arrived at Little Hole and were met by the others who were already there, we were hustled into a waiting van and brought back to the dam again. I told my husband that I wanted to go back to the cabin, that I was through with river running forever. He wisely said, "No, you're not. If you don't go again right now, you will be too afraid to try it again the next year when we come."

He finally convinced me that we must go again, and we did, this time in a tight, safe-looking, large black raft, which proved to be a delight in comparison. I am very thankful for a husband who knew what to do in this situation and made it possible for us to have many more wonderful trips to Flaming Gorge. The camaraderie was wonderful.

This was an annual affair for several years before gas prices went up. Later there were also insurance needs and a greater risk of accidents with so many people involved that made it no longer feasible to go as a ward. However, several families still enjoyed this trip together for many years.

For years, my husband faithfully loaded up our van with wet survivors of the Little Hole experience and hauled them back for a second run down the river. On one of our last trips, he received a special award. The person in charge of the whole trip gave him this award at the program and potluck dinner we always had on Friday night before many left the next day for home. He was given a medal which said, "River Rat," in honor of his service. He treasured that award and all that it meant.

These trips really helped our love and regard for each other as a family. We met challenges and had experiences we surely wouldn't have had just being at home.

10

Bits of Advice for a Happy Marriage

Everyone desires and deserves a happy marriage. To find a good spouse you need to have an open heart and open eyes. After marriage, you needs to keep your eyes half closed.

Several couples or individuals gave such good advice but not in the form of personal stories. Their advice makes up this small chapter.

.❀. ✿ *.❀.*

Be forgiving. Both partners need to be committed to the gospel. Selfishness is perhaps the greatest barrier or problem to a happy marriage.

Have compatible values. Marry the right person, in the right place, at the right time. A temple marriage is one of the deepest and most gratifying of all human relationships but also one of the most demanding.

Be prayerful in the selection of an eternal companion in order to receive confirmation from your Heavenly Father that you are making the proper choice.

Try hard to be organized, to be orderly, and to develop an effective program for self-improvement with goals and objectives. In other words, plan your work and work your plan to include study and learning.

Give your best effort and then be patient with yourself, never losing sight of your goals.

Pay attention to your grooming. Keep yourself neat and attractive!

Be enlightened and interesting.

Recognize that the most important role of a wife will be to create a happy family and a gracious home, no matter how modest it may be.

Accentuate the positive and try to never allow yourself to become discouraged.

Count your blessings (not your money) and be grateful!

Be one with your companion, without losing your identity, and be a strength and a helpmeet to him or her.

Return often to the temple and pay close attention in order to better understand the covenants you have made.

Attitude determines the quality of our lives.

Be grateful!

Set your affection on things above, not on things on the earth.

.❀. ✿ *.❀.*

Both spouses should have input into how their children are raised. Both should be responsible for taking care of those children including child care, bathing, cooking, and taking them to and from school, sports events, and so forth.

Husbands and wives should have some time of their own during each day if possible, or at least each week, to do something they want to do. They should help each other with the children or with other chores so this can happen. Have a night out together once a week if possible or at least once a month. Go to dinner or lunch, to a movie or a ride, or take a walk in the park. Just take some time together away from the children and other friends or family.

Don't jump to conclusions. Make sure you have all the facts.

Be sure to give your spouse a hug and a kiss and tell him or her of your love as soon as you wake in the morning and just before going to sleep at night.

.❀. ✿ *.❀.*

On holidays, especially birthdays, an anniversary, or Christmas, gifts are nice but not essential.

Telling your spouse how much you love and appreciate him or her is important and an essential part of a good marriage.

Put God in your marriage and family life. Build a strong church-oriented family.

Develop good communications between husband, wife, and family. Never put down your spouse or children in front of others.

Emphasizing the positive in disciplining of children will help the husband and wife have a better marriage. Discuss problems privately and not in the presence of the children. Have firm control of young children and gradually release the control so that when they are teenagers they can make good decisions. Time-outs seemed to work for us rather than physical punishments. Deciding how we would discipline our children ahead of time really saved our marriage from many pitfalls.

Avoid selfishness. If either husband or wife is a selfish person, it makes it very hard to have a compatible relationship. The welfare and happiness of the other person should be of utmost importance to each.

Respect is the foundation of love. When both mates are honest, kind, and not controlling, with no abusive actions or feelings, the marriage can be wonderful.

Here are some guidelines for a fulfilling and happy life from one who has been there:

- Have faith in and follow Jesus Christ. It will bring you eternal happiness.
- Love and listen to your spouse.
- Have a second honeymoon at least once a year.
- Take time to teach and enjoy your children. They are a lot more important than a clean house and yard. Think: "How much can I give?" not "What can I get?"
- Buy only that which you can afford. Don't envy others.
- Seek for and follow the promptings of the Holy Ghost.
- Be a "bebigaler" and not a "belittler." Look for the doughnut and not the hole.
- Be a helpful and concerned neighbor.
- Listen to good music. Read good books. Engage in stimulating conversation.
- Be a participant, not just a spectator. Don't be afraid to say "I'll try."

- Don't expect perfection of anyone until you have personally achieved perfection.
- Make a contribution in your work or any assignment you accept. Give credit to others. Show appreciation and compliment others.
- Work is a blessing and not a curse.
- Be an honest person.
- Plant some pansies every spring and get your hands into the soil.
- Own a popcorn popper and an ice cream freezer (and use them).
- Enjoy being alive!

List of Contributors

..* ✿ *.*.*

Alison Affeltranger
Marian Allen (deceased) by
    husband Lewis Allen
Ellis and Carolyn Allred
Muriel Allridge
Jerry Anderegg
Christine Ball
Marcella Barrett (deceased) by
    sister Richine Johnson
Helen Bassett
Janet Bates
Mac Bay
Sharon Beck
Beverly Bruening
Michael Burnett
George I. Cannon
Laurie Carruth
Bryan Carter
Darlene Christensen
Linda Conners
Vaughn Cox
Zella Dahlquist
Dale Dallon
Verda Dallon
Enid Davis

Clayton Fairbourn
Rosemary Fairbourn
Hans and Ruth Froelke
Donna Gebbler
Ann Greenwood
Ronald Greenwood
Lu and Lamont Henriksen
Eugene and Ruth Hilton
David Kezerian
Fay Klingler
Janice Larson
Alan Layton
Margaret Little
Brandi Loffgren
Darin and Maren Lythgoe
Julie McGuire
D'Anna Miller
Roland Nebeker
Susan Nebeker
Gordon Pehrson
Ruth Ann Pehrson
Beverly Petersen
Lorna Pollard
Linda Potter
Don Poulter

David Richardson
Lawrence and Martha
    Richardson
Ray and Pat Richens
Sarah Ripplinger
Sherrie and Bob Rudy
Mirielle Ruppe
Machelle Schade
Michelle Schmidt
Merrill Scott
Madeleine Scoville
Carma Sirrine
David Sirrine
Erika Sirrine
Gordon Sirrine
Jeanay Sirrine
Linda Sirrine
Steven Sirrine

Josie Soderborg
Ida Sorenson
Jan Strong
Merle Sudbury
Gayle Thompson
Larry and Amaryllis Tippetts
Janet Tolman
Lynn Wallace
Jill Wells
Kris Wilfert
Barbara Williams
Elaine Wilson, (deceased) by
    husband Arvil Wilson
Tina Wilson
Susan Winters
Marilyn Wooley
Lowell and Elaine Wright
Elain Young

About the Author

.❀.❁*.❀.*

Carma B. Sirrine was born March 2, 1934, in Price, Utah. She was raised by a loving mother and father in Wellington where her father was a teacher and principal of the school there. She has enjoyed writing since the eighth grade when she wrote a play and several short stories for her English class. In college at Carbon Junior College in Price, she wrote for the school magazine and newspaper, and was associate editor of the yearbook during her sophomore year. She graduated with an Associate of Science degree and then moved to Salt Lake City to find a secretary position. There she met her husband.

After their marriage Carma was a stay-at-home mom for twenty-three years. Over the years she has held many church positions including being a president of the MIA (or Young Women as it is called now), a counselor in Relief Society and primary presidencies, a member of the service and activities committee of the MIA, a Blazer B leader for her ward and stake for several years, and a family history consultants for many more years.

In 1999 she and her husband served a senior mission in Manila, Philippines for nineteen months, to help the members with their livelihood. They had many wonderful and enjoyable experiences there which they will never forget. While in the Philippines, Carma wrote an article for the *Liahona* regarding a special humanitarian project and one regarding a fair held at a large park where the locals sold their wares. These are in the February and November 2000 issues respectively.